BAUMBERGER & STEGMEIER

De aedibus

Der italienische Architekt und Architekturtheoretiker Aldo Rossi verglich die Architektur mit den Wissenschaften. Wie diese schreite die Architektur voran, indem sie stetig auf bereits Erreichtes aufbaue und sich so weiterentwickele. Diesem wissenschaftlichen Aspekt dient diese Buchreihe. Seit 2000 dokumentiert sie die aktuelle Schweizer Architektur. Die Reihe wird in ihrer Kontinuität gleichsam zu einem Gedächtnis der Architektur, das die Werke dem Vergessen entzieht. Von jedem der mit hohem Qualitätsanspruch ausgewählten Architekten und Architektenteams werden die wichtigsten Bauten festgehalten, ausführlich dargestellt und dokumentiert. Jeder Band dient auch der Reflexion über den architektonischen Willen, der hinter den Projekten steht. So sind in dieser Reihe mehr oder minder alle in der Schweiz wirkenden Architekturkritiker mit einzelnen oder mehreren Textbeiträgen vertreten.

    Der Hauptteil in jedem Band widmet sich dagegen der Welt der Anschauung. So sind jeweils anhand von Bildern und Plänen einige bemerkenswerte Bauten dargestellt, die nicht einer routinierten «Produktion» entsprungen sind. Vielmehr steht hinter jedem Entwurf eine leidenschaftliche Auseinandersetzung mit der Aufgabe und deren Prämissen.

De aedibus

The Italian architect and architectural theoretician Aldo Rossi compared architecture to the sciences. Like them, architecture progresses by constantly building upon what has already been achieved and develops further in this way. Since 2000, this series of books has been dedicated to the same academic approach in documenting contemporary Swiss architecture. It therefore becomes a form of architectural memory, ensuring that the architecture is not forgotten. The most important buildings by each of the selected high-quality architects are presented, described in detail and documented. Each volume also serves to reflect upon the architectural motivation behind the projects. By now, more or less every architectural critic working in Switzerland has contributed one or more articles to the series.

    However, the core of each book is dedicated to the world of observation. Images and plans present a number of remarkable buildings that are not the result of routine "production". Instead, each design stems from a passionate engagement with the task and its premises.

De aedibus

BAUMBERGER & STEGMEIER

QUART

Tibor Jonelly
DINGE ANEINANDER VORBEI VERBINDEN 6

HAUS WEHRLI, ZOLLIKON 14

MEHRFAMILIENHAUS SEGANTINISTRASSE, ZÜRICH-HÖNGG 18

PRIMARSCHULZENTRUM, LAUFEN 22

WOHNSIEDLUNG BRÜGGLIÄCKER, ZÜRICH-SCHWAMENDINGEN 28

SCHULANLAGE DORF, DIETLIKON 32

WOHNÜBERBAUUNG AM KATZENBACH III–V, ZÜRICH-SEEBACH 36

WOHNÜBERBAUUNG GUGGACH, ZÜRICH-UNTERSTRASS 42

MULTIFUNKTIONALES WOHNHAUS, OETWIL AM SEE 46

WOHNSIEDLUNG TOBLERSTRASSE, ZÜRICH-FLUNTERN 48

MEHRFAMILIENHAUS OTTIKERSTRASSE, ZÜRICH 54

WOHNÜBERBAUUNG AM CHATZEBACH, MURI 56

LOKSTADT, WINTERTHUR 58

WOHNSIEDLUNG SCHWAMENDINGER-DREIECK, ZÜRICH-SCHWAMENDINGEN 62

FELDMÜHLEAREAL, RORSCHACH 64

Christoph Baumberger
DIE WAHRNEHMUNG IM GEBRAUCH UND DER GEBRAUCH DER WAHRNEHMUNG 66

WERKVERZEICHNIS 74

BIOGRAFIEN, AUSZEICHNUNGEN, BIBLIOGRAFIE 78

Tibor Jonelly
WEAVING THINGS PAST EACH OTHER — 7

WEHRLI HOUSE, ZOLLIKON — 14

SEGANTINISTRASSE APARTMENT BUILDING, ZURICH HÖNGG — 18

PRIMARY SCHOOL CENTRE, LAUFEN — 22

BRÜGGLIÄCKER HOUSING ESTATE, ZURICH SCHWAMENDINGEN — 28

DORF SCHOOL FACILITY, DIETLIKON — 32

AM KATZENBACH III–V HOUSING DEVELOPMENT, ZURICH SEEBACH — 36

GUGGACH RESIDENTIAL DEVELOPMENT, ZURICH UNTERSTRASS — 42

MULTIFUNCTIONAL RESIDENTIAL BUILDING, OETWIL AM SEE — 46

TOBLERSTRASSE HOUSING ESTATE, ZURICH FLUNTERN — 48

APARTMENT BUILDING OTTIKERSTRASSE, ZURICH — 54

AM CHATZEBACH HOUSING DEVELOPMENT, MURI — 56

LOKSTADT, WINTERTHUR — 58

SCHWAMENDINGER-DREIECK HOUSING ESTATE, ZURICH SCHWAMENDINGEN — 62

FELDMÜHLEAREAL, RORSCHACH — 64

Christoph Baumberger
PERCEPTION DURING USE AND USING PERCEPTION — 67

LIST OF WORKS — 75

BIOGRAPHIES, AWARDS, BIBLIOGRAPHY — 79

DINGE ANEINANDER VORBEI VERBINDEN

Tibor Joanelly

Ortstermin in der Lokstadt Winterthur, im Mock-up auf der Baustelle. Ein Ausschnitt des Hauses im Massstab 1:1 zeigt alle wichtigen Details, Anschlüsse und Oberflächen, aussen wie innen. Das Mock-up ist ein eigenes, auf die wesentlichen Entwurfsfragen geschrumpftes Bauwerk: ein Haus, das nur dazu da ist, die konstruktive und materielle Essenz zu demonstrieren, zu bestimmen und zu erproben. Das Mock-up repräsentiert vieles, das in diesem bescheidenen Versuch über die Arbeit eines Architekturbüros verhandelt wird. Zuerst: Aus dem Konzentrat spricht die langjährige Erfahrung von Peter Baumberger und Karin Stegmeier beim Bauen, das Wissen um Fallgruben und mögliche Wirkungen – und natürlich auch um die Möglichkeiten. Dieses Nichthaus, diese Nichtarchitektur ist gut gemacht, ihr ist viel abverlangt, die wenigen Elemente erzielen eine erstaunliche räumliche und materielle Vielfalt.

Mock-up Lokstadt Winterthur

In diesem kleinen Nichthaus stehen also 15 Personen dicht gedrängt und beraten über die Farbe des Bodenbelags: Bauherren, Bauherrenberater, Unternehmer, Generalunternehmer, Architekten, Bauleiter und der Architekturkritiker, dessen Aufgabe es ist, diesen Text zu verfassen. Es ist faszinierend, wie die verschiedenen Stimmen trotz Baulärms ein Gespräch finden, faszinierend, wie diszipliniert dieses Gespräch abläuft und wie schnell man zu einer Einigung kommt. Interessant ist es auch zu beobachten, wie Baumberger permanent moderiert, mit Gelassenheit. Ein bisschen ist das wie im Fernsehen oder auf einem Podium: Hinter Rolle und Argument verschwindet die Person. Unaufgeregt, routiniert und sachlich werden die Codewörter des Bauens ausgetauscht. Irgendwann dann fasst Baumberger zusammen: «Der Antrag wäre somit klar.» Man ist froh, die Gruppe eilt zum nächsten Ortstermin, der Bemusterung eines Treppenhauses.

Besichtigung Mock-up Lokstadt Winterthur
Mock-up viewing, Lokstadt Winterthur

Es ist auch interessant nachzuvollziehen, wie es zu dieser Einmütigkeit kommt. In ihrem Herbeiführen scheint eine eigene Strategie des Büros im Umgang mit den Bedingungen des Bauens zu liegen. Dabei geht es offenbar darum, die Dinge stets in der Schwebe zu halten und eine klare Linie zu finden, die zwischen allen Unwägbarkeiten des Bauens hindurchführt zu einer Form, die kontrolliert erscheint und architektonisch wirkt. Baumberger & Stegmeier scheinen in ihrer Arbeit stets von Gegebenem auszugehen, von dem, was eine Aufgabe ausmacht und bestimmt. Vom Kontext. Das Entwerfen der beiden Architekturschaffenden gleicht eher einem Suchen als einem Setzen. In diesem Prozess erstaunt, mit welcher Sicherheit etwa Baumberger vorgeht, sowohl in der Argumentation als auch in der Moderation. «Die Diskussion ist jetzt offen», so Baumberger. Dabei ist ja eigentlich alles schon festgelegt.

Das Wort «Kontext» wird in diesem Text eine wichtige Rolle spielen, vielleicht entgegen den in der Vorbesprechung genannten Absichten. Kontext ist in der Schweizer Architektur der letzten 20 Jahre sozusagen die «eierlegende Wollmilchsau». Der Kontext muss irgendwie immer alles begründen. Meine Generation von Architekturschaffenden ist diejenige, die ohne Kontext kaum entwerfen kann.

Die Bemusterung des Treppenhauses der Lokstadt ist dafür eine Lektion. Das Gespräch dreht sich um die Farben von Beton und Stahltreppe, dabei findet es mit den bereits erwähnten Beteiligten in einer Industriehalle statt, deren Farbgebung aus der Zeit der erfolgreichen Maschinenindustrie den Kontext für die Farbwahl vorgibt. Baumberger vernetzt seine Argumentation immer wieder von Neuem – das Wort «vernetzen» wird in diesem Text ebenfalls eine Rolle spielen. Wiederholt wird ein Bemühen

WEAVING THINGS PAST EACH OTHER

Tibor Joanelly

Mock-up Zentrumsentwicklung Geroldswil
Mock-up, Geroldswil centre development

A meeting in the Lokstadt, Winterthur, inside the mock-up on the building site: a section of the building with a 1:1 ratio presents all the important details, connections and surfaces, both outside and inside. The mock-up is a building in its own right, shrunk down to the key design problems; a house that is only there to demonstrate and test its structural and material essence. The mock-up represents many things that are discussed in this modest essay on the work of an architectural office. Firstly: the concentrated structure expresses the many years' experience of Peter Baumberger and Karin Stegmeier in construction, their knowledge of pitfalls and possible consequences – and of course also all the contingencies. This non-house, this non-architecture is well made. Much is demanded of it. The few elements achieve a surprising spatial and material diversity.

So, in this non-house, 15 people crowd together and discuss the colour of the flooring: the client, the client's advisor, the contractor, the general contractor, the architects, the building manager, the philosopher writing in this book and the architectural critic, whose task it is to write this text. It is fascinating how the different voices become a discussion despite the noise of the construction work, how disciplined that discussion is and how quickly an agreement is reached. It is also interesting to observe how Baumberger constantly guides the dialogue with serenity – a little like a TV talk show or panel discussion: his person disappears behind his role and argument. The code words of building are exchanged calmly, routinely and professionally. Eventually, Baumberger sums up: "The proposal is therefore clear." The group is happy and everyone hurries to their next on-site appointment to sample the staircase.

It is also interesting to see how such unanimity is achieved. It seems to be a particular strategy of the architectural office to engage with the condition of building. The apparent focus lies on keeping things undetermined while also following a clear line that leads between all unforeseeable aspects of building, moving towards a form that appears to be controlled and yet architectonic. In their work, Baumberger & Stegmeier always seem to start from the already given, from what defines and determines a task. Their design resembles an act of searching rather than positioning. In this process, Baumberger for instance advances with surprising self-assurance, both in his arguments and in his mediation. "The discussion is now open," Baumberger declares. Actually, everything has already been determined.

The word "context" will play an important role in this text, perhaps also going against the intentions mentioned in discussions before it was written. Context has become a kind of all-purpose weapon in Swiss architecture of the last 20 years. Context must somehow justify everything. My generation of architects can hardly design without a context.

The sampling of stairs for the Lokstadt is a lesson in this respect. The discussion centres on the colour of the concrete and steel stairs and is attended by the above-mentioned participants in an industrial hall. Its colour refers back to the period of successful machine industry and defines the colour range for selection. Baumberger regularly networks his arguments with new

deutlich, das Gesagte mit der bisherigen Argumentation und mit dem Ort der Referenz, an dem man steht, in Beziehung zu setzen – es zu kontextuieren.

Dasselbe Vorgehen von Baumberger anlässlich eines weiteren Ortstermins, bei der Besichtigung der Siedlung Brüggliäcker in Zürich-Schwamendingen. Auch dort geht es um die Kontextuierung, die Vernetzung der Themen des Entwurfs in der Umgebung bis hin zur Farbe: Grün als Chiffre für die Architektur der 1950er-Jahre, die das Quartier prägt. Doch die Farbe etwa der Fensterläden, typische Elemente der Gartenstadt, erscheint verfremdet: nicht wertkonservativ, sondern avantgardistisch. Le Corbusiers Grün als weitere Referenz, als eine weitere Vernetzung des Architekturentwurfs.

Mock-up Wohnsiedlung Brüggliäcker
Mock-up, Brüggliäcker housing estate

Warum an dieser Stelle das Verb «vernetzen»? Zum einen ist es ein passendes Synonym für die Architektur und auch die Arbeit Architekturschaffender, denn das Bauen hat metaphorisch und nicht selten wirklich etwas mit der Tätigkeit des Webens zu tun. Dinge müssen aneinander vorbei gefügt werden. Und weil Architekturschaffende heute vor allem in gegebenen Kontexten arbeiten, so erhält die Metapher zugleich eine städtebauliche und kulturelle Bedeutung. Sie besagt, dass verbunden, geflickt, eingewoben wird. Zudem werden Ideen in die Textur unseres Lebensraums eingewoben.

Beim Vernetzen oder Verweben – oder wie auch immer man die Tätigkeit des Entwerfens nennen möchte – spielt der innere Widerstand der Dinge eine wichtige Rolle: das, was gleich bleibt, und das, was verändert werden kann. So finden die Dinge unter der Moderation der Architekturschaffenden zusammen und bleiben dabei sie selbst: Das Grün von Le Corbusier in der Gartenstadt ist das Grün von Le Corbusier. Das Industriehallengelb im Treppenhaus ist das Gelb der Industriehalle. Struktur und Veränderung finden nicht nur in der Metapher des Webens zusammen, sondern auch im Prozess des Vermittelns von Ideen, als Gesetztes und Offenes: Als Beteiligter fühlt man sich nur durch den Kontext eingegrenzt und nicht durch den Willen oder die Absichten der Projektierenden.

Baumberger & Stegmeier halten ihre Argumentationen offen. Sie loten aus, sind neugierig auf alle gesellschaftlichen Bereiche. Beim Entwerfen möchten sie nichts ausschliessen, sie wollen Realitäten zusammenführen: Bauherren, Ökonomie, Recht und Bewohner. Das Verweben dieser verschiedenen Realitäten hat zugleich etwas von einem Teppich, dessen Textur und Bildhaftigkeit immer dichter und genauer werden: «Und am Schluss stimmt es, am Schluss möchte man darin wohnen», so Stegmeier.

Der Prozess dieses Zusammenführens von Bedingungen und von thematischen Strängen beginnt schon ganz am Anfang des Entwerfens. Anlässlich eines weiteren Ortstermins im Büro wird dies klar. An der Projektsitzung eines der Wettbewerbsteams muss erst einmal das Gipsmodell erweitert werden, Baumberger möchte mehr über den Kontext erfahren. Die Mitarbeiter haben also das Gipsmodell etwas improvisiert um etwa die Hälfte mit Styropor und zerknülltem Skizzenpapier vergrössert, und die dadurch gewonnene Information ist sehr viel präziser, als sie scheint. Denn mit der «Befragung» des ergänzten Modells mittels darauf abgelegter Styroporbaukörper – die vorerst nicht viel mehr sind als Typen – ergeben sich erste Begriffsfelder, welche die Schwierigkeiten und Chancen der Entwurfsaufgabe umreissen. Der Sitzung vorausgegangen sind Varianten. Jede hat auf dem Untersuchungsfeld des Gipsmodells eine grundsätzlich verschiedene Haltung festgelegt.

Diese Haltung gegenüber der Aufgabe ist die Ausgangslage für den Entwurf. Sie wird deutlich, sobald sich die wichtigsten Parameter der Aufgabe in Worte fassen lassen und somit für den Entwurf und seine Kommunikation verfügbar werden. Aus

aspects – the word "networking" will play another role in this text. There is a clear, repeated effort to create a reference between what is said and the argumentation to date, as well as to contextualise this reference in the current location.

The same approach was evident in Baumberger's discourse during another on-site visit at the Brüggliäcker estate in Zurich Seebach. In this case, too, the contextualisation and interlinking of the design's themes in the surroundings goes as far as the colour: green is a reference to the architecture of the 1950s that characterised the neighbourhood. However, the colour of the window shutters for instance, which are typical elements of a garden city, appears to be alienated: instead of expressing conservative values, they seem avant-garde. Le Corbusier's green is another reference that further networks the architectural design.

Why use the word "networking" here? Firstly because it is an appropriate synonym for architecture and the work of its designers, since building has a metaphorical and often also a real connection to the activity of weaving. Things must be woven past each other. And since today's architects above all work in given contexts, the metaphor also gains an urban-planning and cultural significance. It states that things are joined, patched and woven. Even ideas are intertwined into our environment.

When networking or interweaving – or however one wishes to call the activity of designing – the inner resistance of things plays an important role: what remains the same and what can be changed. Under the auspices of architects, things are brought together and nevertheless remain themselves: the green of Le Corbusier in the garden city is the green of Le Corbusier. The yellow colour of the industrial halls is still the yellow of the industrial halls when used in the staircase. Structure and change do not only come together in the metaphor of weaving, but also in the process of mediating ideas – as something that is set and yet open. As a participant in the discussion, one only feels limited by the context, not by the will or intention of the architects.

Baumberger & Stegmeier keep their argumentation open. They sound out, are curious about social aspects; when designing, they do not wish to exclude anything, instead preferring to bring together realities: clients, economics, law and residents. Interweaving these different realities also has to do with a carpet, its texture and imagery becoming ever denser and more precise: "And finally, it is right. Ultimately, one wants to live there," as Stegmeier puts it.

This weaving together of conditions and thematic strands already begins at the start of the design process. It becomes clear at a further visit to their offices. At a project meeting of one of the office's competition teams, a plaster model must first be expanded, since Baumberger wishes to know more about the context. So the employees improvise somewhat on the plaster model, enlarging it by about half with styrofoam and crumpled sketch paper. The information gained in this way is far more precise than at first appears. The "investigation" of the enlarged model using styrofoam building volumes placed upon it – which are initially little more than types – produces the first field of terms that outline the difficulties and opportunities of the design task. Different versions were produced before the meeting. Each determined a fundamentally different attitude towards the studied area of the plaster model.

den Schlüsselbegriffen wird oft später dann der Wettbewerbstext entwickelt, der meist schon in der ersten Recherche angelegt ist.

Das, was Baumberger & Stegmeier als «Haltung» bezeichnen, ist in den zum Abschluss eines Entwurfs mitgelieferten Texten nicht selten mit dem Modalverb «soll» gekennzeichnet: «…Aussenräume sollen am ‹Gartenteppich› der umliegenden Grundstücke anknüpfen», es «soll mit zunehmendem Abstand vom Gebäude die private Nutzungsintensität abnehmen», in der Freiraumgestaltung «sollen Gartenmauern eine tragende Rolle spielen». Das suggestive Soll sorgt in einem grundsätzlich schwierig zu steuernden Projektprozess für Verbindlichkeit bei gleichzeitiger Offenheit. Die Argumente, die einem Entwurf zugrunde gelegt werden sollen, sind verhandelbar und doch bindend. Deutlich wird dies etwa, wenn in einem Wettbewerbstext davon die Rede ist, dass ein Projekt «eine Bebauungsstruktur mit Solitärbauten sucht».

Mock-up Wohnüberbauung Guggach
Mock-up, Guggach housing development

«Suchen» ist ein weiteres potentes Verb, und es ist wiederum bezeichnend für die Arbeit von Baumberger & Stegmeier: Denn das «Verweben» der Argumentationen gleicht von Anfang an einer Suchbewegung, bei der ein Hauptargument umkreist wird. Baumberger greift dabei im Entwurfsgespräch gewisse Argumente zu materiellen Gegebenheiten immer wieder neu auf, rekapituliert das bisher Erkannte. So verfestigen sich die Gedanken.

Entscheidend an diesem Vorgehen ist, dass die Erkenntnis, wie bereits angedeutet, stets in der Schwebe gehalten wird. Das ist ganz im Sinne von Richard Sennetts Verständnis vom Handwerk als einem generellen Bezug zur Welt, bei dem implizites Wissen durch Zögern, Umwege und vorsichtiges Abwägen entsteht. Interessant ist paradoxerweise, dass damit die in der Deutschschweizer Architektur mittlerweile etwas hohle Formel des Kontexts mit Inhalt gefüllt werden kann. Denn das langsame Erkennen und Begreifen bringt ein kontinuierliches Aufgreifen vorhandener Strukturen mit sich, von Strukturen, die dann im Entwurf an Bedeutung gewinnen und deren tragende Beständigkeit eben als Haltung, als zu erreichender Zustand formuliert wird. Das Wort «Strukturen» ist hier viel präziser als das unter Architekturschaffenden gebräuchliche Wort «Bezüge».

Natürlich verwenden Baumberger & Stegmeier auch Referenzbilder, man sieht sie im Atelier an die Wand gepinnt. Doch diese spielen im frühen Entwurfsstadium eine eher untergeordnete Rolle, wollen mehr Denkräume sein als eng geführte Analogien. Sie dienen als Lieferanten von Argumenten, welche die Entwurfsaufgabe verständlicher und begreifbar machen. Später dann, wenn der Entwurf voranschreitet, sind Bilder für die formale Umsetzung und die Kommunikation im Projektteam nützlich. Doch kein Bild trumpft mit Wiedererkennbarkeit auf über die im Kontext gefundenen Begebenheiten. Derart bleibt das Endresultat stets auch für Laien nachvollziehbar und wirkt nicht abgehoben.

Man könnte all das hier Beobachtete vielleicht Ausdruck einer «realistischen Haltung» nennen. Ich meine dies in dem Sinn, dass das Entwerfen nicht auf entwurfsbestimmenden Fiktionalisierungen beruht, es sind eher die materiellen Begebenheiten eines Kontexts, die Baumberger & Stegmeier interessieren: der topografische Verlauf etwa, die Vegetation, die Aussicht, bestehende Wege, der Lärm und in einem städtischen Kontext etwa die Beschaffenheit der umgebenden Bebauung und die sie umschliessenden Räume – sowohl im Sinne von Proportionen als auch von absoluter Grösse. Dazu gehören Überlegungen zu Vermietbarkeit, Gebrauch und Gewohnheit.

Derart kontextuiert unterliegt ein Entwurf durchaus dem sogenannten Wysiwyg-Prinzip, das man aus der Sprache der Benutzeroberflächen im digitalen Zeitalter kennt:

Mock-up Wohnsiedlung Toblerstrasse, Etappe I
Mock-up, Toblerstrasse housing estate, phase I

This attitude towards a task is the starting point for a design. It becomes clear as soon as the most important parameters can be defined in words and thereby made available to the design process and its communication. Competition texts are often developed out of the key terms later on and are thereby already established during the initial research process.

What Baumberger & Stegmeier describe as attitude is often expressed with the modal verb "should" in the text delivered at the end of the design process: "exterior spaces should adjoin with the 'garden carpet' of the surrounding properties," or, "the private use intensity should be reduced with increasing distance from the building," or, "garden walls should play a key role," with respect to the design of open spaces. The suggestive "should" ensures the statement's binding nature in a project process that is fundamentally difficult to steer, while also being open. The arguments on which a design will be based are negotiable and yet binding. This becomes clear when a competition text declares that a project "*seeks* a development structure with free-standing buildings".

"To seek" is another powerful verb and is again characteristic of the work of Baumberger & Stegmeier: from the outset, the "weaving" of different arguments is like a searching movement, circling around a main argument. During the design discussions, Baumberger repeatedly picks up new aspects of certain arguments on the material conditions, recapitulating what is already known. Ideas are consolidated in this way.

The decisive aspect in this approach is that knowledge, as already indicated in this text, remains in balance. This is entirely in keeping with Richard Sennett's understanding of craftsmanship as a general reference to the world, in which implicit knowledge is made available through hesitation, detours and careful weighing up. Paradoxically, it is interesting to note that the formula of context, which has become somewhat hollow in German-speaking Swiss architecture, can be filled with content in this way. For the slow process of recognition and comprehension entails continuously picking up on existing structures, which then gain in significance in the design and whose fundamental stability is formulated as an attitude, a goal that should be aimed for. The word "structures" is much more precise in this context than the word "references", which is commonly used among practising architects.

Naturally, Baumberger & Stegmeier also use reference images and one can see them pinned to the wall in their studio. However, they play a subordinate role in the early stages of design and are intended more as thinking spaces than as strict analogies. They serve as providers of arguments that make the design task more understandable and tangible. Later, as the design is progressing, images are useful for implementation and communication within the project team. Yet no image has a higher priority in terms of recognisability than the conditions that can be found in the project's context. This ensures that the final result can always be grasped by non-professionals and is not too aloof.

One could perhaps describe everything observed in this way as a "realistic stance". I mean it in the sense that the design is not based on fictionalisations that define its concept. Instead, Baumberger & Stegmeier are interested in the material conditions of a context: including topographical features, vegetation, the view, existing paths, noise and, within an urban context, the nature of the surrounding buildings and the spaces that envelope it – both in the sense of

What you see is what you get. Erkennbar wird diese Haltung nicht nur bei der Siedlung Brüggliäcker, doch dort in aller Deutlichkeit. Die sichtbaren Teile der Baukörper sind maximal einfach konstruiert, nichts ist versteckt, nichts minimalisiert wie in den 1990er-Jahren, nichts ist «wegdetailliert». Alle Teile sind stumpf gefügt, nichts ist beschönigt.

Auch für die Siedlung Brüggliäcker wurde ein Mock-up angefertigt. Mittlerweile, so Baumberger, habe man «eine beachtliche, dokumentierte Sammlung an solchen kleinen Häusern beisammen». Vielleicht werde ein weiteres Buch daraus. Wie auch immer: Die Mock-ups symbolisieren einen eigenen Kontext der Arbeit von Baumberger & Stegmeier, nämlich denjenigen, den ihre Architektur selbst schafft, ein Konzentrat, ihre Substanz. Dabei sind die Mock-ups in keiner Weise Architektur – längst sind sie Raum. Die Faszination, die diese Gebilde einem Betrachter abnötigen, macht sie zu einem eigenen Werk, abhängig von Entwurf und Bauprozess zwar, aber doch mit eigenen Qualitäten, nicht weit entfernt von einer Kunstinstallation. Hier irgendwo also muss eine essenzielle und doch geheime Verbindung zwischen Bauen und Kunst bestehen.

Mock-up Wohnsiedlung Schwamendinger-Dreieck, fotografiert von David K. Ross für die Serie *Archetypes* (ständige Sammlung des Canadian Center for Architecture)
Mock-up, Schwamendinger-Dreieck housing estate, photo by David K. Ross for the series Archetypes (permanent collection at the Canadian Center for Architecture)

proportions and in terms of absolute size. They also include aspects of rentability, use and habits.

Contextualised in this way, such a design certainly conforms to the so-called "WYSIWYG" principle that is well known in the field of computer science and user interfaces in today's digital age: what you see is what you get. This attitiude is not only evident in the Brüggliäcker estate, but also particularly clear there. The visible parts of the building volumes are construed in the simplest possible way, nothing is hidden or minimised, as it used to be in the 1990s. Nothing is made invisible by detailing. All parts are coarsely joined, nothing is embellished.

A mock-up was also produced for the Brüggliäcker estate. According to Baumberger, "a considerable, documented collection of such small houses has been assembled in the meantime". Perhaps it will lead to a book one day. Whatever the case: the mock-ups symbolise another specific context of the work of Baumberger & Stegmeier, namely the context their architecture itself creates – its concentrate, its substance. The mock-ups are by no means architecture – yet they certainly do frame space. The fascination that these formations hold for the viewer makes them works in their own right, independent of the design and the building process, but nevertheless with their own qualities that are not far removed from installation art. So perhaps, an essential and yet secret connection between building and art must exist somewhere within them.

WEHRLI HOUSE, ZOLLIKON

The initial situation of this project was a villa built in 1929, which was to be converted into an apartment building with three spacious flats. Careful interventions to the architecture preserved the building's expression despite the conversion and extension measures.

The new extension accommodates two bedrooms with a bathroom on the ground floor and a large, bright eat-in kitchen on the upper level, including a terrace in front of it. The roof was converted into a three-room apartment with a lucarne, offering a view of the lake. The ceilings on the attic level, which are individual, steeply rising pointed domes, give the rooms additional height and create a specific spatial situation.

The existing building has "national romantic" style elements, such as the ornate main entrance, the playfully offset windows and structured, unobtrusive building cubatures, as well as classic modern elements, such as the loggia to the south east, which connects volumetrically to the main building. Like the existing loggia, the new extension also forms a counterpart to the main building. However, the two are connected by sculptural staggering in a vertical direction.

The offset apertures in the northwestern façade open up an area and highlight the building volume despite their dimensions. At the same time, the window divisions establish a relationship with the existing building in terms of their scale. The façade of sand-blasted concrete also has a similar colour and grain to the plaster façade of the original building, combining the two building volumes into a unity.

Direct contract, 2005
Project: Extension and conversion of a villa into three apartments
Client: private
Construction: 2007

Tent room, Schloss Charlottenhof Potsdam, Karl Friedrich Schinkel, 1826–1829

Site plan 1:5000

Grundriss Erdgeschoss 1:150
Ground floor plan 1:150

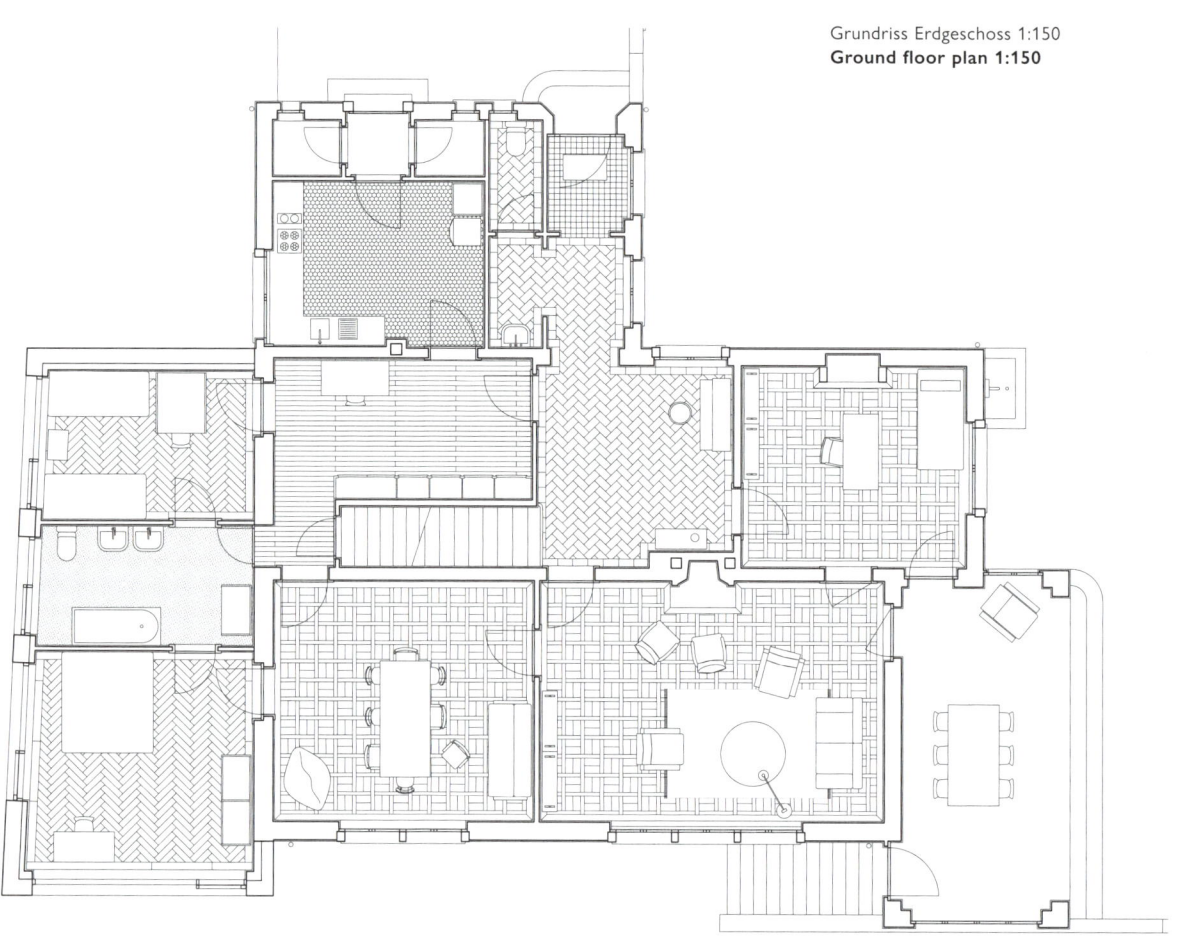

Schnitt 1:200
Sectional view 1:200

MEHRFAMILIENHAUS SEGANTINISTRASSE, ZÜRICH-HÖNGG

SEGANTINISTRASSE APARTMENT BUILDING, ZURICH HÖNGG

Das Grundstück befindet sich an privilegierter Lage am Hönggerberg mit Blick über die Stadt und die Berge. Anstelle eines Einfamilienhauses sollte dort ein repräsentatives Haus mit vier Eigentumswohnungen entstehen. Der Neubau fügt sich präzise in die Topografie ein und nimmt durch das Knicken des Volumens die Massstäblichkeit des Orts auf. Trotz höherer Dichte gelingt die Neuinterpretation des Themas eines Wohnhauses im Privatgarten: Die Wohnungen verbinden die Ideale des Einfamilienhauses – Privatheit und Gartenbezug – mit denjenigen einer städtischen Geschosswohnung.

In allen Wohnungen ist ein Grundrisstypus mit klarer Trennung von öffentlichen und privaten Bereichen verschieden ausformuliert. Entsprechend den unterschiedlichen Raumgeometrien, der Aussicht und der Lage der privaten Aussenräume sowie dem Bezug zum Garten wurden differenzierte Grundrisse mit individuellen Qualitäten entwickelt. Thematisch knüpft der Wohnungsbau mit seinen genau determinierten Räumen und Bewegungsfiguren an den Reichtum bürgerlicher Wohnkultur der Nachkriegsmoderne an.

The property is situated in an attractive location on the Hönggerberg with a view over the city and the mountains. The single-family home there was to be replaced by a prestigious building with four owner-occupied apartments. The new building is precisely integrated into the topography and is buckled to assume the scale of the location. Despite the high density, the new interpretation succeeds in expressing the theme of a residential building in a private garden: the apartments combine the ideals of a single-family home – privacy and a reference to the garden – with those of a multi-storey urban apartment.

In all apartments, a basic floor plan type that clearly distinguishes between public and private areas is formulated in different ways. The differentiated floor plans were developed with individual qualities according to the varying spatial geometries, the view and the placement of the private exteriors, as well as the reference to the garden. Thematically, the apartment building, with its precisely determined spaces and movement figures, picks up on the diversity of post-war bourgeois residential culture.

Direktauftrag 2006
Projekt: Neubau, Wohnhaus mit 4 Eigentumswohnungen
Bauherr: privat
Ausführung: 2008–2010

Direct contract, 2006
Project: New residential building with four owner-occupied apartments
Client: private
Construction: 2008–2010

Mehrfamilienhaus in Stuttgart von Chen Kuen Lee, 1961
Apartment building in Stuttgart by Chen Kuen Lee, 1961

Terrassenhaus: Haus Schminke in Löbau von Hans Scharoun, 1933
Terraced house: Schminke House in Löbau by Hans Scharoun, 1933

Situation 1:5000
Site plan 1:5000

Grundrisse Erdgeschoss, 1.–3. Obergeschoss 1:250
Floor plans, ground floor and 1st–3rd floors 1:250

PRIMARSCHULZENTRUM, LAUFEN

PRIMARY SCHOOL CENTRE, LAUFEN

Das Schulareal liegt auf einer Terrasse am Hang gegenüber dem Stadttor des mittelalterlichen Stadtkerns von Laufen. Die bestehenden Schulhäuser aus verschieden Zeiten reihen sich auf der schmalen Fläche parallel zum Hang auf. Der Neubau erweitert dieses heterogene Ensemble und schliesst es nach Osten hin ab. Mit seinem Mehrzwecksaal dient er neben der Schulnutzung zugleich als öffentliches Gebäude. Kern der städtebaulichen Idee war es, auf dem Schulareal einen für die Bevölkerung nutzbaren öffentlichen Stadtplatz zu schaffen, der über den Pausenplatz hinaus in der tiefer liegenden, witterungsgeschützten Mehrzweckhalle seine räumliche Fortsetzung findet. Das Schulareal erhielt dadurch eine Aufwertung zu einem wichtigen Begegnungsraum für die Gemeinde.

Die Schule verbindet sich mit ihren Innenhöfen und Aussenbezügen mit dem Grünraum und den Gärten der Umgebung. Der Neubau versteht sich dabei als eine über den Turnhallensockel gelegte Pavillonstruktur: Das auf einen Fachwerkträger und zwei Schrägstützenachsen aufgelegte, als Faltwerk ausgebildete Dach gliedert das Obergeschoss und dient als Tragwerk für die abgehängten Zwischenauflager der Geschossdecken. Dies ermöglicht die effiziente Überbrückung der grossen Spannweite der Doppelturnhalle ohne zusätzliche Unterzüge.

Die kleinteilige Gliederung des Faltdachs wie auch der Fassade gibt dem grossen Baukörper die Massstäblichkeit der Umgebung und lässt im Innenraum eine einzigartige Dachlandschaft entstehen. Der gestockte Jurakalkbeton und das Jurakalkbrüstungsband im Obergeschoss spiegeln die Geschichte des Orts als Steinbruch wider und gliedern den Neubau in die Reihe der Bestandsbauten ein.

The school grounds are situated on a terrace on a slope opposite the gate to the medieval town centre of Laufen. The existing school buildings from different periods are lined up on this narrow area parallel to the slope. The new building extends the heterogeneous ensemble and concludes it to the east. With its gymnasium, which is also used as a multifunctional hall, it serves public purposes as well as its school uses. The core of the urban planning idea was therefore to create a public urban space on the school grounds that could be used by residents, and which is spatially continued in a lower, sheltered area in the multifunctional hall. The school grounds were thereby enhanced into an important public area.

The school, with its inner courtyards and external references, combines with the surrounding green spaces. The new building is conceived as a pavilion structure placed upon the base that accommodates the gymnasium: the roof, which is supported by a trussed beam and two diagonal support axes and consists of a folded-plate, structures the upper level and serves as a load-bearing structure for the suspended interior supports of the intermediate floors. This enables efficient spanning of the large distance of the double gymnasium without additional joists.

The small-scale structure of the folded-plate roof, as well as the façade, allows the volume to adapt to the scale of the town and creates a unique interior roof landscape. The stamped Jurassic limestone concrete and the Jurassic limestone balustrade band on the upper storey reflect the location's quarrying history and structure the new buildings within the row of the existing buildings.

Offener zweistufiger Projektwettbewerb 2007, 1. Preis
Projekt: Neubau, Primarschulhaus mit 6 Klassenzimmern, 2 Kindergärten und einer Doppelturnhalle als Mehrzwecksaal
Bauherr: Stadt Laufen
Ausführung: 2009–2013

Open, two-stage project competition in 2007, 1st Prize
Project: New construction of a primary-school building with 6 classrooms, 2 kindergartens and a double gymnasium as a multifunctional hall
Client: Municipality of Laufen
Construction: 2009–2013

Pavillonteppich mit Innenhöfen: Munkegaard-Schule in Genthofte im Norden Kopenhagens von Arne Jacobsen, 1957
Carpet of pavilions with inner courtyards: Munkegaard School in Genthofte in the north of Copenhagen by Arne Jacobsen, 1957

Laufener Altstadt mit Schulareal im Hintergrund
Laufen old town with the school grounds in the background

Steinbruch in Laufen, 1920
Quarry in Laufen, 1920

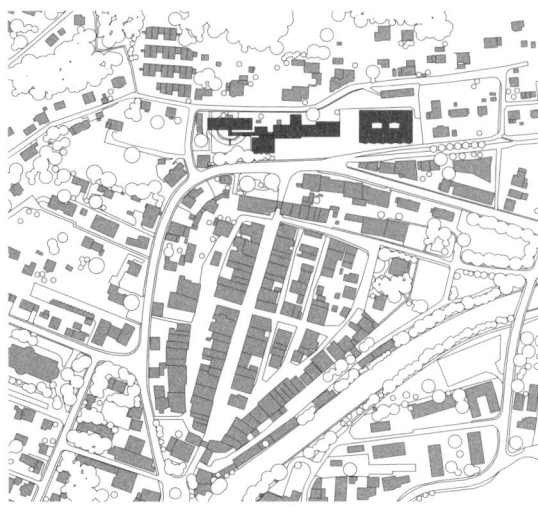

Situation 1:7500
Site plan 1:7500

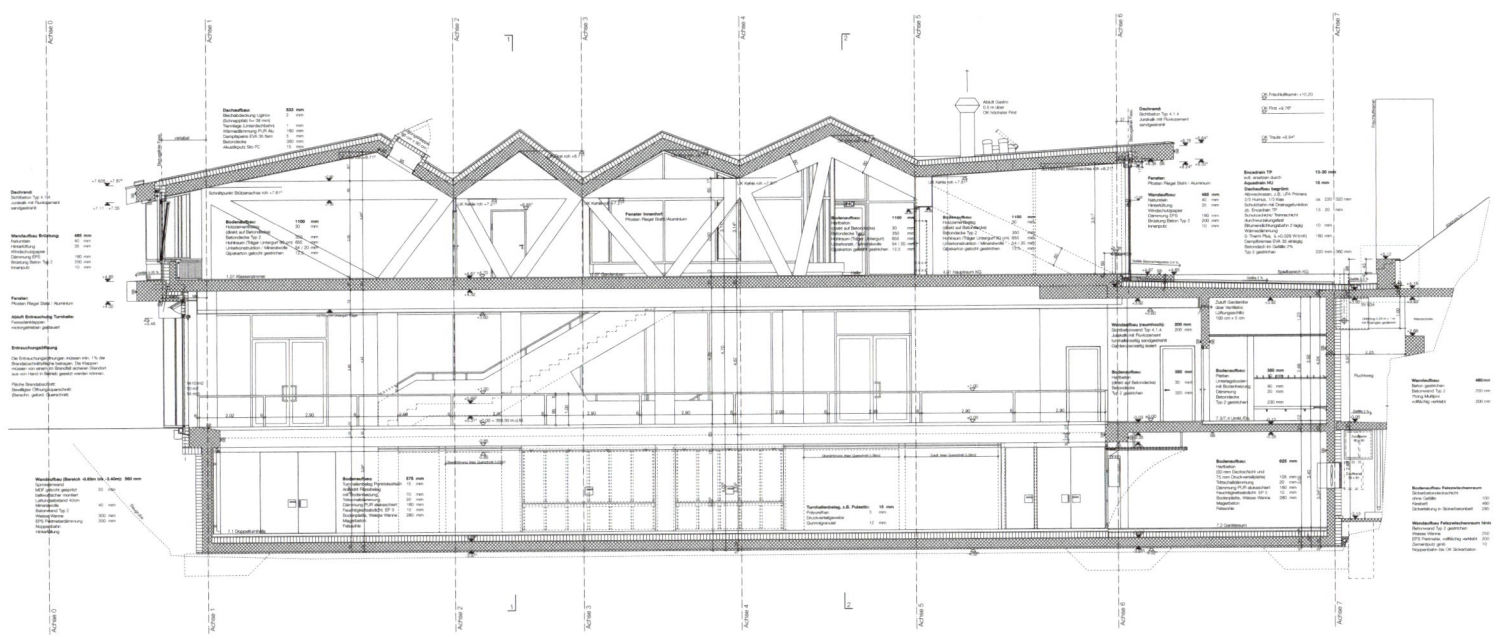

Konstruktionsschnitt
Sectional view of the structure

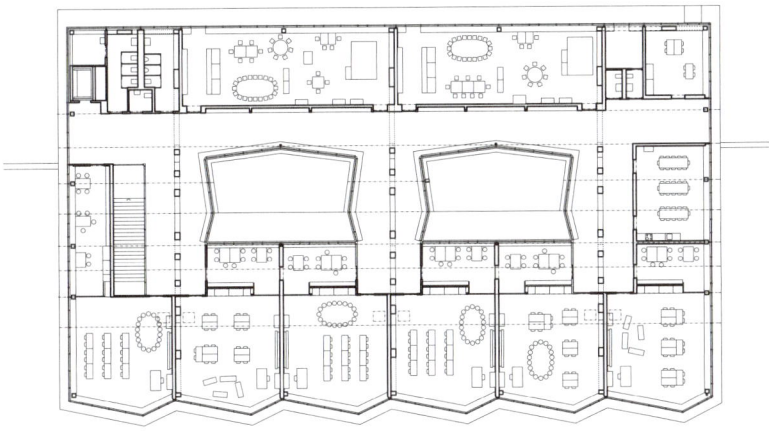

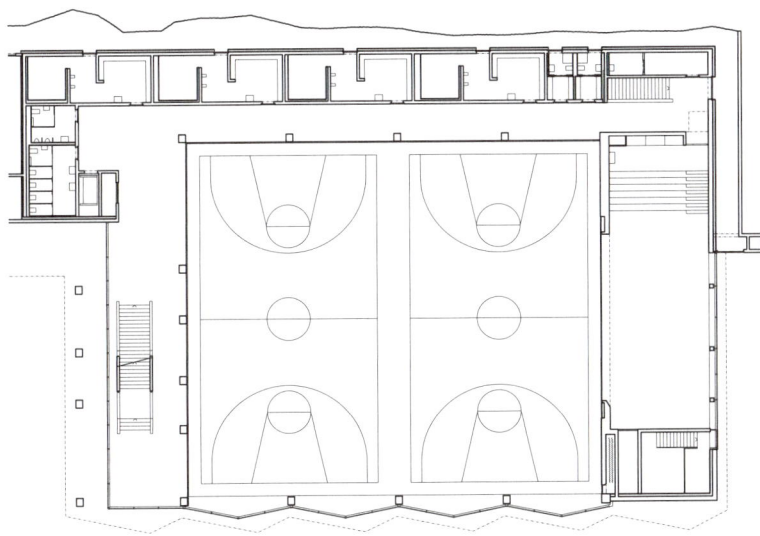

Grundrisse Ober- und Erdgeschoss 1:1200
Floor plans, upper level and ground floor 1:1200

WOHNSIEDLUNG BRÜGGLIÄCKER, ZÜRICH-SCHWAMENDINGEN / BRÜGGLIÄCKER HOUSING ESTATE, ZURICH SCHWAMENDINGEN

Die Wohnsiedlung Brüggliäcker befindet sich am Übergang von Oerlikon zu Schwamendingen, an der Nahtstelle von einem kleinteiligem Einfamilienhausquartier und den Zeilenbauten der Gartenstadt Albert Heinrich Steiners. Die dreigeschossigen Baukörper übernehmen die Höhe der umliegenden Häuser und verweben sich durch die in die Tiefe gestaffelte Aussenräume mit dem Grünraum der Umgebung. Die Figur der Baukörper lässt sich in ihren tatsächlichen Dimensionen von keinem Standpunkt aus erfassen, wodurch eine dem Quartier entsprechende Massstäblichkeit und Intimität entsteht.

Die Wohnungsgrundrisse entwickeln sich aus wechselseitigen Aussenraumbezügen. Die lang gestreckten Wohnungen spannen sich mit den offen gegliederten Wohn- und Essräumen zwischen den beiden Gartenräumen auf und sind zweiseitig, die Kopfwohnungen dreiseitig orientiert. Die Wohnungen verfügen über individuell nutzbare Räume und ermöglichen vielfältige Wohnformen.

Die beidseitig vorgelagerten Lauben sind als grosszügige, private Aussenräume ausgebildet und nehmen, als eigentliche Gartenzimmer, die Idee vom Wohnen in der Gartenstadt auf. Entsprechend sucht das Projekt in seiner Materialisierung inhaltlich und stimmungsmässig eine Verwandtschaft zu den 1950er-Jahre Bauten des Gartenstadtquartiers. Die Häuser sind mit einer hinterlüfteten, vertikalen Holzschalung verkleidet und teils schwedenrot teils lichtgrau gestrichen. Diese an den Gebäudekanten wechselnde Farbigkeit bricht die Grösse des Volumens mehrfach und vermittelt mit der Massstäblichkeit des umliegenden Kontexts.

The Brüggliäcker residential estate is situated at the transition between Oerlikon and Schwamendingen, representing the threshold between a neighbourhood of small-scale single-family homes and the housing rows of Steiner's garden city. The three-storey volumes assume the height of the surrounding buildings and interweave with the surrounding green spaces by means of exterior spaces with staggered depths. The figure of the buildings cannot be grasped in its entire dimensions from any one perspective, creating an appropriate scale and intimacy for the neighbourhood.

The apartment floor plans develop out of the mutual relationships with the exterior space. With their openly structured living and dining areas, the elongated apartments stretch between the two garden spaces and have exposures on at least two – or in the case of the end units, three – sides. The apartments have individually usable rooms, allowing various forms of living.

The arbours on both sides are designed as generous, private exterior spaces and pick up on the idea of living in a garden city, in effect acting as garden rooms. Accordingly, the project's materialisation seeks a relationship to the 1950s buildings in the garden-city quarter, both in terms of its content and its atmosphere. The buildings there are clad in a back-ventilated, vertical wooden casing and painted partly in Swedish red and partly in light grey. The colours, which alternate at the building edges, repeatedly break down the size of the volume and mediate with the scale of the surrounding context.

Projektwettbewerb mit Präqualifikation 2009, 1. Preis
Projekt: Ersatzneubauten mit 70 Wohnungen
Bauherr: BAHOGE Wohnbaugenossenschaft, Zürich
Ausführung: 2009–2014
Zusammenarbeit: Edelaar Mosayebi Inderbitzin Architekten (BS+EMI Architektenpartner), Zürich
Landschaftsarchitektur: Hoffmann & Müller Landschaftsarchitektur, Zürich

Project competition with prequalification, 2009, 1st Prize
Project: Replacement buildings with 70 apartments
Client: BAHOGE Wohnbaugenossenschaft, Zurich
Construction: 2009–2014
Collaboration: Edelaar Mosayebi Inderbitzin Architekten (BS+EMI Architektenpartner), Zurich
Landscape architecture: Hoffmann & Müller Landschaftsarchitektur, Zurich

Wohnsiedlung Auzelg von Cramer & Jaray & Paillard, 1952–1954
Auzelg housing estate by Cramer & Jaray & Paillard, 1952–1954

Modell Wohnsiedlung Brüggliäcker
Model, Brüggliäcker housing estate

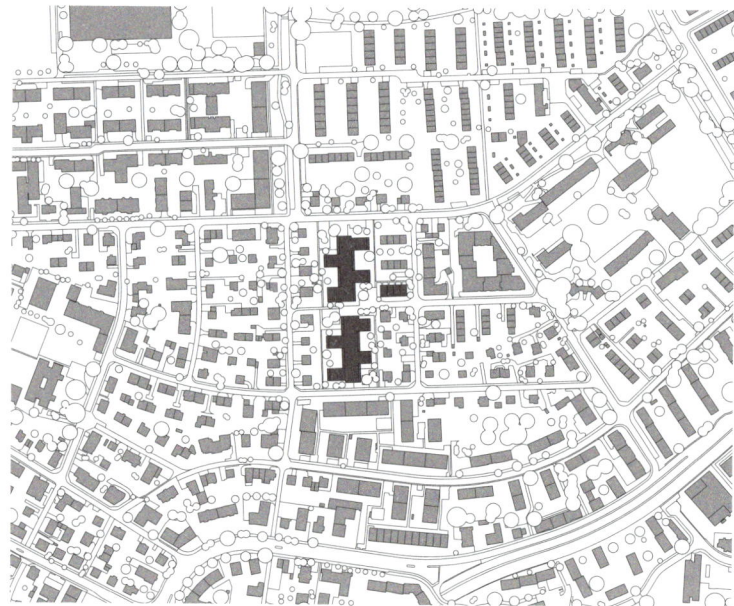

Situation 1:7500
Site plan 1:7500

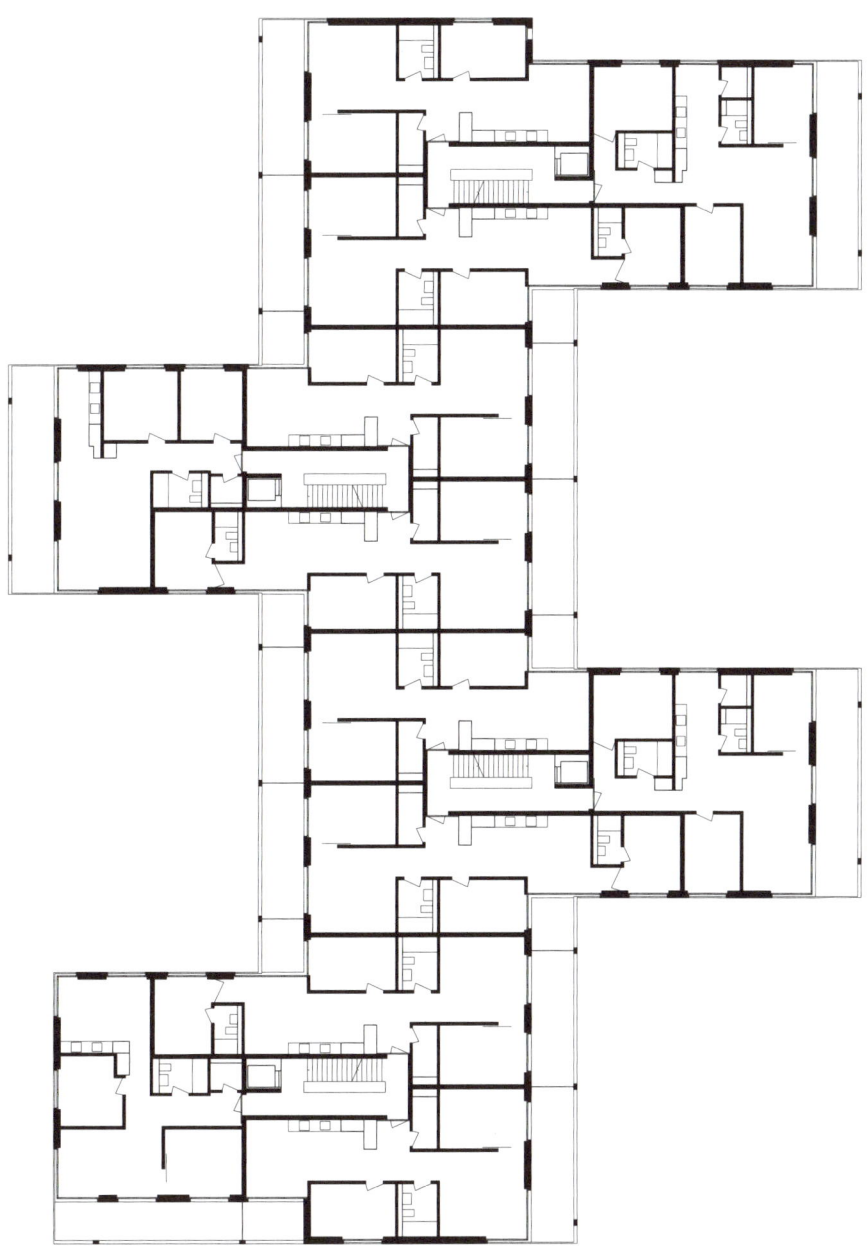

Grundriss Regelgeschoss 1:400
Standard floor plan 1:400

SCHULANLAGE DORF, DIETLIKON
DORF SCHOOL FACILITY, DIETLIKON

Das Schulhausareal Dorf befindet sich am Rand des alten Dorfkerns von Dietlikon. Der zweigeschossige Neubau beherbergt sechs Grundstufenzimmer und die neue Gemeindebibliothek. Mit den beiden bestehenden Schulhäusern fasst er einen Hof, der als Pausenplatz dient.

Über den zweigeschossig gedeckten Eingangsbereich, der durch das weit auskragende Vordach und den Sockel gebildet wird, gelangt man in die Eingangshallen. Diese dienen gleichzeitig der Erschliessung mit Garderoben, Aufenthaltsräumen, einem Zugang zum Garten und einem gedeckten Aussenbereich. Vier Grundstufenzimmer befinden sich im Erdgeschoss, zwei im Obergeschoss des Neubaus. Jeweils zwei Schulzimmer mit Gruppen- und Materialräumen, einem Lehrerzimmer und Nasszellen bilden eine Einheit.

Der Zugang zur Bibliothek im Obergeschoss erfolgt über den baumbestandenen Platz im Süden des Areals. Der Bibliothekssaal öffnet sich komplett an den Längsseiten des Gebäudes und gewährt Ausblicke zum Pausenplatz und in die Umgebung.

Die Grösse des Neubaus lässt ihn massstäblich für den Ort und für seine Nutzer erscheinen. Die Verwendung des ortsüblichen Baustoffs Holz bindet das Haus darüber hinaus in seine Umgebung ein. Die mit vertikalen Holzlamellen verkleidete Fassade ermöglicht durch ihr Spiel mit offenen und geschlossenen Elementen Durch- und Einblicke: Das Haus wirkt leicht und transparent. Ein lichtgrauer, seidenglänzender Anstrich verleiht dem Holzbau Abstraktion und fügt ihn optisch mit den beiden vorhandenen Schulbauten zu einer Einheit zusammen.

The grounds of the Dorf school facility are situated on the edge of the old village centre of Dietlikon. The two-storey new building accommodates six primary school classrooms and a new municipal library. Together with the two existing school buildings, it frames a yard that is used as a playground.

Visitors reach the entrance halls via the two-storey covered entrance area, which is formed by the broadly projecting canopy and the base. These also serve to provide distribution, with cloakrooms and common rooms, as well as access to the garden and a covered exterior area. Four primary classrooms are situated on the ground floor of the new building, with a further two on the upper level. Each unit includes two classrooms with group and material rooms, a teacher's office and sanitary units.

The library on the upper level is accessed via the leafy square in the southern part of the grounds. The library room completely opens up along the longitudinal sides of the building, providing views of the playground and the surroundings.

The size of the new building gives it an appropriate scale for the location and its users. The use of the locally traditional building material of timber also connects the building to its surroundings. The façade, which is clad in vertical wooden slats, enables views through and into the building due to the interplay between open and closed elements, making the building seem light and transparent. A light grey, silk-glossy paint gives the timber building an abstract quality and combines it with the two other existing schools to create a unity.

Offener Projektwettbewerb 2008, 1. Preis
Projekt: Umbau bestehender Schulanlage «Dorf» und Neubau mit 6 Grundstufenzimmern und Bibliothek
Bauherr: Schulgemeinde Dietlikon
Ausführung: 2011–2014
Landschaftsarchitektur: Atelier Garten und Wohnen, Dietlikon

Open project competition in 2008, 1st Prize
Project: Conversion of the existing Dorf school facility and new construction of 6 primary classrooms and a library
Client: Dietlikon School Community
Construction: 2011–2014
Landscape architecture: Atelier Garten und Wohnen, Dietlikon

Schulhaus Probstei in Zürich von Albert Heinrich Steiner, 1946–1951
Probstei School building in Zurich by Albert Heinrich Steiner, 1946–1951

Bauernhaus aus Ostermundigen von 1797, Freilichtmuseum Ballenberg
Farmhouse from Ostermundigen, built in 1797, Ballenberg open-air museum

Stalldurchfahrt, weiss gekalkt
Whitewashed stable drive

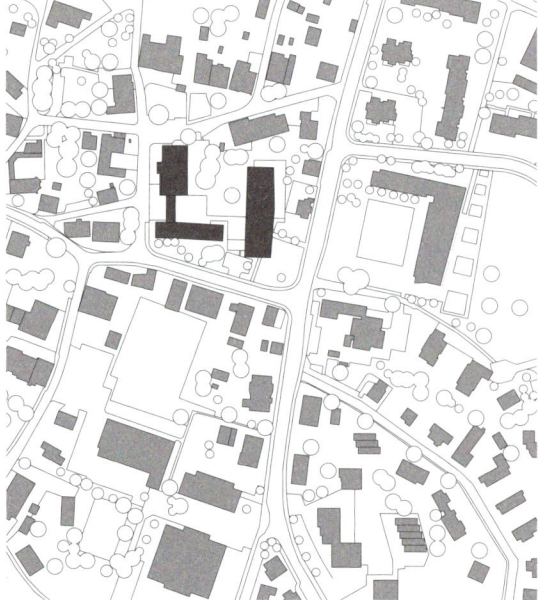

Situation 1:5000
Site plan 1:5000

QUART

HIGHLIGHTS

2020/1

www.quart.ch

Peter Märkli – Everything one invents is true

Peter Märkli zählt seit den frühen 1980er-Jahren zweifellos zu den markantesten Deutschschweizer Architekten der ersten Stunde. Seine einprägsamen Bauten lassen sich jedoch nicht leicht in das Schema dieser Architekturbewegung einordnen. Zu sehr sind die einzelnen Bauwerke intensiv bearbeitete Individuen, die einer fortdauernden Bewegung des Suchens folgen. Immer eröffnen sie eigenständig und eindringlich Verbindungen der Geschichte der Architektur mit dem Impetus einer zeitüber-dauernden Gültigkeit.

Im vorliegenden Band sind 17 Bauten der letzten 15 Jahre mit Texten, Plänen und Abbildungen ausführlich dargestellt. Ergänzt wird die bemerkenswerte Werkdarstellung mit erhellenden Essays von Florian Beigel & Philip Christou, Franz Wanner und Ellis Woodman. Ein spannendes Interview mit Peter Märkli von Elena Markus und einzelne Statements des Architekten runden die eindrückliche Sammlung ab.

Herausgegeben von Pamela Johnston
Textbeiträge: Florian Beigel & Philip Christou, Pamela Johnston, Peter Märkli, Elena Markus, Franz Wanner, Ellis Woodman

240 Seiten, 29 × 29 cm
178 Abbildungen, 75 Pläne,
101 Zeichnungen
Hardcover, fadengeheftet
Englisch (teilweise übersetzt ins Deutsche *):
ISBN 978-3-03761-138-8
Englisch (teilweise übersetzt ins Japanische **):
ISBN 978-3-03761-139-5
CHF 138.– / EUR 126.–
* eingelegtes Booklet mit Essays in Deutsch
** eingelegtes Booklet mit Projektbeschrieben in Japanisch

Peter Märkli – Everything one invents is true

Since the early 1980s, Peter Märkli has been one of the most striking protagonists of German Swiss architecture from the earliest period of its emergence. However his impressive buildings cannot be easily classified in the scheme of this architectural movement, since the individual buildings are intensely developed individuals that follow the continuous movement of seeking. They always open up connections with the history of architecture in an independent, powerful way and express the impetus of timeless validity.

This volume presents 17 buildings in detail from the last 15 years with texts, plans and images. The remarkable presentation of works is complemented by enlightening essays by Florian Beigel & Philip Christou, Franz Wanner and Ellis Woodman. An exciting interview with Peter Märkli by Elena Markus and individual statements by the architects round off the impressive collection.

Edited by: Pamela Johnston
Articles by: Florian Beigel & Philip Christou, Pamela Johnston, Peter Märkli, Elena Markus, Franz Wanner, Ellis Woodman

240 pages, 29 × 29 cm
178 illustrations, 75 plans,
101 sketches
Hardback, thread-stitched
English (some texts also in German *):
ISBN 978-3-03761-138-8
English (some texts also in Japanese **):
ISBN 978-3-03761-139-5
CHF 138.00 / EUR 126.00
* with an enclosed booklet containing the essays in German
** with an enclosed booklet containing the project texts in Japanese

Einzelausgabe / Individual edition

Zürcher Wohnungsbau 1995–2015

Seit Mitte der 1990er Jahre lässt sich im Grossraum Zürich eine ausserordentliche Qualität von Wohnbauten beobachten. Durch die Förderung der öffentlichen Hand, durch eine hochstehende Wettbewerbskultur und eine rege Architekturszene ist hier ein reichhaltiges Experimentierfeld guter Wohnbauarchitektur entstanden. Das umfangreiche Werk über den Zürcher Wohnungsbau ist eine Anthologie von über 100 Einzelbauten, Ensembles und Siedlungen, die innerhalb von 20 Jahren in der Stadt Zürich entstanden sind. Es ist eine eindrückliche Übersicht zur Wohnbaukultur, die mit ihrer aussergewöhnlichen Qualität eine Intensität und Blüte erlebt, die auch internationale Beachtung findet.

Herausgeber: Heinz Wirz, Christoph Wieser

Zurich Housing Development 1995–2015

Housing of exceptional quality has been developed in the greater Zurich area since the mid-1990s. Public funding, the high standard of the competition culture and a vibrant architectural scene have resulted in a rich field of experimentation for good residential architecture. The approximately 500-page volume on Zurich housing construction is an anthology of over 100 individual buildings, ensembles and settlements developed over a period of 20 years. It is an impressive representation of an intense, blossoming housing development culture that has also attracted international attention.

Edited by: Heinz Wirz, Christoph Wieser

476 Seiten, 24 × 29 cm
710 Abbildungen, 713 Pläne
Hardcover, fadengeheftet
Deutsch/Englisch
ISBN 978-3-03761-127-2
CHF 138.– / EUR 126.–

476 pages, 24 × 29 cm
710 illustrations, 713 plans
Hardback, thread-stitched
German/English
ISBN 978-3-03761-127-2
CHF 138.00 / EUR 126.00

Monografie / Monograph

Gion A. Caminada

Von Gion A. Caminada ist in der bündnerischen Surselva ein architektonisches Werk entstanden, das wie kein anderes unmittelbar in den ökonomischen, geografischen und bautechnischen Prämissen eines Ortes und den Lebensgewohnheiten seiner Bevölkerung bedingt ist.
Die neue Buchausgabe umfasst die Texte und die Projektsammlung des Bandes Cul zuffel e l'aura dado und ist erweitert um eine Auswahl der neueren Projekte seit 2005.

Herausgegeben von: Bettina Schlorhaufer
Fotos: Lucia Degonda
Textbeiträge: Gion A. Caminada, Jürg Conzett, Bettina Schlorhaufer, Peter Schmid, Martin Tschanz, Peter Rieder, Walter Zschokke

Gion A. Caminada

Gion A. Caminada has produced architectural work in Surselva, Grisons that is unique in being directly determined by the ecological, geographical and structural engineering premises of the location and the lifestyles of its population.
The new edition includes the texts and project collection of Cul zuffel e l'aura dado and is extended to include a selection of more recent projects since 2015.

Herausgegeben von: Bettina Schlorhaufer.
Fotos: Lucia Degonda. Textbeiträge: Jürg Conzett, Peter Schmid, Peter Rieder, Walter Zschokke

2., mit neuen Projekten erweiterte Auflage des Bandes Cul zuffel e l'aura dado

296 Seiten, 22,5 × 29 cm
296 Abbildungen, 214 Skizzen/Pläne
Hardcover, fadengeheftet
Deutsch/Englisch
ISBN 978-3-03761-114-2
CHF 138.– / EUR 126.–

2nd edition of Cul zuffel e l'aura dado, extended to include new projects

296 pages, 22.5 × 29 cm
296 illustrations,
214 sketeches/plans
Hardback, thread-stitched
German/English
ISBN 978-3-03761-114-2
CHF 138.00 / EUR 126.00

81 Frei Rezakhanlou

Mit der Schulanlage von Chermignon im Unterwallis ist den beiden Lausanner Architekten Eric Frei und Kaveh Rezakhanlou 2010 auf einen Streich eine ausserordentliche Anlage gelungen, die wie eine griechische Tempelanlage die Kraft hat, Landschaft, Topografie, Stadtmorphologie und Gebäudetypus zu vereinen. Daneben realisieren die Architekten weitere Projekte in hoher architektonischer Qualität.

104 Seiten, 22,5 × 29 cm, 111 Abbildungen, 50 Pläne
Fadengeheftete Broschur, CHF 48.– / EUR 44.–
Deutsch/Englisch ISBN 978-3-03761-206-4

Simple, spacious buildings and clearly structured interior arrangements characterise the buildings by this Geneva team of architects led by Philippe Meier. They are volumes for a range of building tasks, such as the Oncology Centre and a Business School in Geneva, or the renovation and extension of a media library in Sion.

104 pages, 22.5 × 29 cm, 111 images 50 planss
Stitched brochure, CHF 48.00 / EUR 44.00
German/English ISBN 978-3-03761-206-4

82 L-architectes

Zwei Architektinnen, Jeanne Della Casa und Sylvie Pfaehler, zusammen mit ihren neuen Partnern Michael Perret und Lucile Fonta-Rak, arbeiten in Lausanne an einem bemerkenswerten Werk. Drei Wohnbauten in Holz inmitten eines städtischen Gartens und ein Ensemble von Wohnbauten strahlen eine eigene Poesie aus. Zu ihren ausgezeichneten Werken zählen auch tektonisch klar gegliederte Wohnbauten in Lausanne und in der Lavaux.

92 Seiten, 22,5 × 29 cm, 61 Abbildungen, 28 Pläne
Fadengeheftete Broschur, CHF 48.– / EUR 44.–
Deutsch/Englisch ISBN 978-3-03761-112-8
Deutsch/Französisch ISBN 978-3-03761-219-4

Two architects, Jeanne Della Casa and Sylvie Pfaehler, together with their new partners Michael Perret and Lucile Fonta-Rak, are working on a remarkable oeuvre in Lausanne. In the midst of an urban garden and an ensemble of housing, three timber residential developments have their own poetic radiance. The architects' award-winning works include clear tectonically structured residential buildings in Lausanne and the Lavaux region.

92 pages, 22.5 × 29 cm, 61 images, 28 plans
Stitched brochure, CHF 48.00 / EUR 44.00
German/English ISBN 978-3-03761-112-8
German/French ISBN 978-3-03761-219-4

42 Inches Geleta

Der Architekt Matteo Inches und die Architektin Nastasja Inches-Geleta in Locarno entwerfen seit 2012 erlesene Bauten, die jeweils ganz aus der Atmosphäre des Orts und der nahen Umgebung entwickelt sind. Mit einer ausgesprochenen Affinität zu Konstruktion und räumlichem Ausdruck sind die bemerkenswerten Bauten stimmig in den baulichen Kontext eingebunden.

48 Seiten, 16,5 × 21 cm, 22 Abbildungen, 25 Pläne
Fadengeheftete Broschur, CHF 28.– / EUR 25.–
Deutsch/Englisch ISBN 978-3-03761-207-1

Since 2012, the two Locarno architects Matteo Inches and Nastasja Inches-Geleta have been designing a number of exquisite buildings, each developed entirely out of the atmosphere of the location and the nearby surroundings. With an exceptional affinity to construction and spatial expression, the impressive structures are concisely integrated into the continuum of the context.

48 pages, 16.5 × 21 cm, 22 images, 25 plans
Stitched brochure, CHF 28.00 / EUR 25.00
German/English ISBN 978-3-03761-207-1

18 Schulz und Schulz – Leipzig

Die Brüder Ansgar Schulz und Benedikt Schulz stellen in diesem Band ihr beeindruckendes Werk vor. Es sind kraftvolle, plastische Figuren mit präziser städtebaulicher Setzung, die in der Materialität, im Typus, in ihren Formen und ihrem Ausdruck stimmig in das Kontinuum des Kontexts eingebunden sind.
Textbeitrag: Katharina Benjamin

64 Seiten, 22,5 × 29 cm, 95 Abbildungen, 28 Pläne
Fadengeheftete Broschur, CHF 48.– / EUR 44.–
Deutsch/Englisch ISBN 978-3-03761-209-5

In this volume, the two brothers Ansgar and Benedikt Schulz present their impressive works: powerful, sculptural figures with precise urban planning placement that are integrated coherently into the continuum of the context through their materials, type, form and expression.

64 pages, 22.5 × 29 cm, 95 images, 28 plans
Stitched brochure, CHF 48.00 / EUR 44.00
German/English ISBN 978-3-03761-209-5

Körper in Räumen

Franziska Wittmann forscht am Lehrstuhl von Gion A. Caminada zu einem Umgang mit physikalischen Naturgesetzlichkeiten und physiologischen Momenten in Architekturen. 2017 wurde das Buch «Leistungen der Architektur» publiziert. Das Ziel dieser Arbeit war es, einen bewirkenden Umgang mit Formen und Materialien aufzuzeigen. In diesem Wissen liegt nicht nur ein Beitrag zur Energieproblematik sondern die Möglichkeit, die Architektur insgesamt mit Qualitäten zu bereichern. Das Buch «Körper in Räumen» knüpft an dieser Stelle an. Im Fokus steht hier nicht die Erzeugung von physikalischen Konstellationen durch die Architektur sondern die Wirkung dieser Zuständen auf den Menschen. Die Publikation stellt gesammelte physiologische Wirkungen so dar, dass sie im Sinne einer reicheren Architektur wirksam anwendbar sind. Die Sammlung zeigt physiologische Phänomene, architektonische Entsprechungen und Beispiele aus der Architekturgeschichte.

Autorin: Franziska Wittmann
Herausgeber: ETH Zürich, Professur Gion A. Caminada

64 Seiten, 14,5 × 29,7 cm
45 Abbildungen und 57 Pläne
Fadengeheftete Freirückenbroschur mit 11 Klappen
Deutsch ISBN 978-3-03761-210-1
Englisch ISBN 978-3-03761-212-5
CHF 43.– / EUR 39.–

Bodies in Spaces

Franziska Wittmann researches at the Chair of Gion A. Caminada on approaches to natural physical laws and physiological factors in architecture. Instead of focusing on the creation of physical constellations through architecture, her work investigates the effects of these conditions on people. The publication presents collected physiological effects in a way that makes them applicable, with the aim of enhancing architecture. The collection presents physiological phenomena, architectural parallels and prominent examples in architectural history.

Author: Franziska Wittmann
Edited by: ETH Zürich Chair of Gion A. Caminada

64 pages, 14,5 × 29,7 cm
45 illustrations and 57 plans
Stitched lay-flat brochure with 11 fold-outs
German ISBN 978-3-03761-210-1
English ISBN 978-3-03761-212-5
CHF 43.00 / EUR 39.00

Analoge Altneue Architektur

Analoge Architektur und Altneue Architektur prägen die Lehre von Miroslav Šik an der ETH Zürich. In der ersten Analogen Phase 1983–1991 assistiert Šik am Lehrstuhl Fabio Reinhart und ist faktisch Wortführer einer architektonischen Bewegung, die weit über die Schweizergrenze hinaus bekannt wird, die bis heute Wirkung zeigt. In der zweiten Altneuen Phase 1999–2018 realisiert Miroslav Šik als Entwurfsprofessor an der ETH Zürich eine Reformarchitektur mit Ensemble, Milieu-Stimmung und Midcomfort. Der umfangreiche Band enthält insgesamt 135 ausgewählte studentische Projekte aus beiden Phasen, deren etliche Verfasser heute zu den namhaften Schweizer Architekten zählen. Grossformatige perspektivische Zeichnungen, Collagen, Pläne mit Detailtreue und prägnant formulierte Projektbeschreibungen veranschaulichen bildhaft die Methode und deren Ergebnisse.

Herausgeber: Miroslav Šik, Eva Willenegger
Textbeiträge: Miroslav Šik, Lukas Imhof, Alberto Dell'Antonio, Andreas Hagmann, Christoph Mathys

Auf der Shortlist des Richard Schlagman Art Book Award 2019

474 Seiten, 21 × 29 cm
694 Abbildungen, 522 Pläne/Skizzen
Hardcover, fadengeheftet
Deutsch ISBN 978-3-03761-153-1
Englisch ISBN 978-3-03761-154-8
CHF 128.– / EUR 116.–

Analogue Oldnew Architecture

The terms "analogue architecture" and "oldnew architecture" are key aspects of the teaching of Miroslav Šik at the ETH Zurich. During his first period there (1983–1991), Šik worked as Senior Assistant at the Chair of Fabio Reinhart and was in effect the spokesman of an architectural movement that became renowned far beyond the borders of Switzerland and is still influential today. Miroslav Šik worked as a Full Professor at the ETH Zurich between 1999 and 2018 during his second period there.
This extensive volume contains the best 135 works respectively by students from both periods of Miroslav Šik's teaching, including plans, project descriptions and perspective diagrams. Some of the presented students went on to become renowned contemporary Swiss architects.

Editor: Miroslav Šik, Eva Willenegger
Articles by: Miroslav Šik, Lukas Imhof, Alberto Dell'Antonio, Andreas Hagmann, Christoph Mathys

Shortlisted for the Richard Schlagman Art Book Award 2019

474 pages, 21 × 29 cm
694 images, 522 plans/sketches
Hardback, thread-stitched
German ISBN 978-3-03761-153-1
English ISBN 978-3-03761-154-8
CHF 128.00 / EUR 116.00

Baumeisterhaus – Käferstein & Meister

Auftraggeber dieses Mehrfamilienhauses an der Ecke Oberwiesenstrasse/Binzmühlestrasse in Zürich-Oerlikon war ein Baumeister. Dieser Umstand ist sinnstiftend für die Architektur des Gebäudes selbst. Sie bezieht sich auf die schlichten, oft mit grosser handwerklicher Eleganz und Solidität ausgestatteten Bauten, die in vergangenen Epochen aus der Werkstatt von Baufirmen im Sinne einer «Architektur ohne Architekten» entstanden sind.

Herausgeber: Heinz Wirz
Textbeitrag: Jonathan Sergison

House for a Builder – Käferstein & Meister

A master builder was the client for this apartment building on the corner of Oberwiesenstrasse and Binzmühlestrasse in Zurich. That situation gives the architecture its character of simple, often accomplished elegance and a solidity of structures that used to be erected by building company workshops in the spirit of an "architecture without architects".

Editor: Heinz Wirz
Article by: Jonathan Sergison

48 Seiten, 16 × 24 cm
17 Abbildungen, 10 Pläne
Fadengeheftete Klappenbroschur
Deutsch/Englisch
ISBN 978-3-03761-200-2
CHF 38.– / EUR 32.–

48 pages, 16 × 24 cm
17 illustrations, 10 plans
Stitched fold-out brochure
German/English
ISBN 978-3-03761-200-2
CHF 38.00 / EUR 32.00

79 Meyer Piattini

Seit 1996 führen Lukas Meyer und Ira Piattini ihr Architekturbüro in Lamone bei Lugano. Inzwischen liegt ein spannendes, reifes Werk vor, das gleichsam die Tessiner «Tendenza» weiterentwickelt. Mit hoher Raffinesse und einer stets mitschwingenden Poesie sind Bauten entstanden wie etwa der Sitz der Credit Suisse in Lamone, ein Verwaltungsgebäude in Monte Carasso oder die sogenannten cinque case in Barbengo.

80 Seiten, 22,5 × 29 cm, 72 Abbildungen, 26 Pläne
Fadengeheftete Broschur, CHF 48.– / EUR 44.–
Deutsch/Englisch ISBN 978-3-03761-189-0

Lukas Meyer and Ira Piattini have been operating from their architectural office in Lamone near Lugano since 1996. By now, they have produced an exciting, mature oeuvre that also represents a further development of the Ticino "Tendenza". Their great sophistication and the constant integration of poetic aspects have contributed to buildings such as the headquarters of Credit Suisse in Lamone, an administrative building in Monte Carasso and the so-called cinque case in Barbengo.

80 pages, 22.5 × 29 cm, 72 images, 26 plans
Stitched brochure, CHF 48.00 / EUR 44.00
German/English ISBN 978-3-03761-189-0

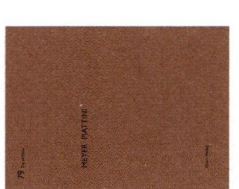

80 weberbrunner

Seit 1999 fallen die Zürcher Architekten Roger Weber und Boris Brunner aufgrund von etlichen Wettbewerbserfolgen immer wieder auf. Ihre Wohnanlagen, Schulen und öffentliche Gebäude sind stets wohlüberlegte, raumhaltige, raumorientierte Lösungen, die mit ausgeprägtem architektonischem Instinkt entworfen sind.

92 Seiten, 22,5 × 29 cm, 123 Abbildungen, 34 Pläne
Fadengeheftete Broschur, CHF 48.– / EUR 44.–
Deutsch/Englisch ISBN 978-3-03761-202-6

Since 1999, the Zurich architects Roger Weber and Boris Brunner have produced an impressive oeuvre based on numerous competition successes. Their residential developments, schools and public buildings are always well-considered, voluminous, spatially orientated solutions designed with a powerful architectural instinct.

92 pages, 22.5 × 29 cm, 123 images, 34 plans
Stitched brochure, CHF 48.00 / EUR 44.00
German/English ISBN 978-3-03761-202-6

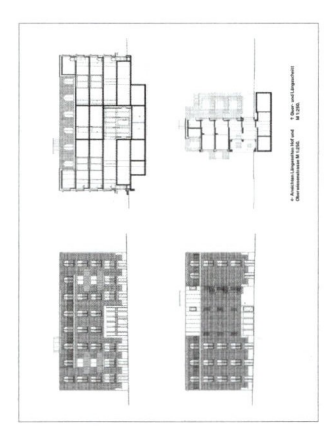
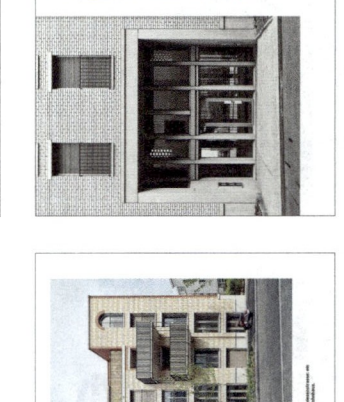

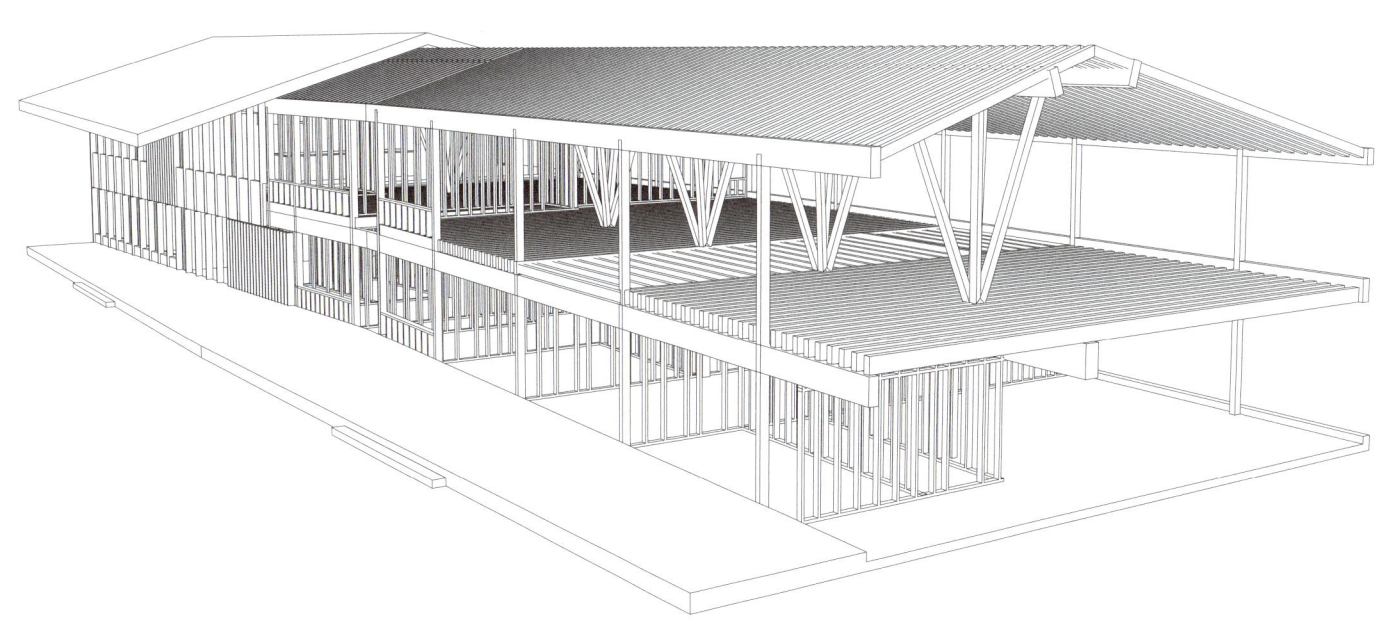

WOHNÜBERBAUUNG AM KATZENBACH III–V, ZÜRICH-SEEBACH

AM KATZENBACH III–V HOUSING DEVELOPMENT, ZURICH SEEBACH

Das Quartier Seebach hat seine Wurzeln in der Ideenwelt der Gartenstadt. Die Ersatzneubauten der genossenschaftlichen Wohnüberbauung am Katzenbach knüpfen daran an.

Die fünf Baukörper der Etappe III weisen lediglich drei Geschosse auf, sind in ihren Grunddimensionen kompakt und suchen eine Fortschreibung der bestehenden Bebauungsstruktur. Die nicht orthogonalen Grundrissgeometrien erzeugen eine spannungsvolle fliessende Räumlichkeit, die durch die Zimmervolumina in einen Eingangs-, Küchen- und Wohnbereich gegliedert wird, Korridore wurden vermieden. Die Häuser sind mit einer hinterlüfteten, in gebrochenem Weiss beschichteten Wellblechfassade bekleidet. Das Relief der Fassadenhaut erzeugt weiche Licht- und Schattenverläufe, die in ihrer Weichzeichnung in Bezug zur umgebenden Vegetation stehen. Im Erdgeschoss schaffen Bodenplatte und Sockel in Sichtbeton den Übergang vom Haus zum Garten.

Die Wohnhäuser der Etappen IV und V bilden eine Stadtkante zum Katzenbachpark im Norden aus. Sie bestehen aus einer Folge von stereometrisch verwandten Körpern, welche sich an die unterschiedlichen Grundstückstiefen anpassen und ausgehend von innenräumlichen Gesetzmässigkeiten ihre Gestalt finden. In den Wohnungen entwickeln sich die Raumfiguren des Wohnens zwischen diesen polygonalen Aussenformen, den nach Süden zum Park orientierten Eckloggien und den rechteckigen Zimmern. Von der Strasse aus werden immer wieder Durchblicke zwischen den Häusern in den Park ermöglicht, die sich in der Wahrnehmung der Passanten unterschiedlich öffnen und schliessen. Mit der dunklen Fassadenverkleidung aus rotbraun glasierten Keramikplatten setzten sich die Gebäude vom Grün des Parks ab.

The Seebach district has its roots in the principles of the garden city. The replacement buildings for the Am Katzenbach residential development pick up on that idea.

The five volumes of stage III only have three floors, compact basic dimensions and seek to continue the existing building structure. The non-orthogonal floor plan geometries create an intense, fluent spatial quality structured by the room volumes, which are divided into an entrance, a kitchen and a living area. Corridors are avoided. The buildings are clad in a back-ventilated corrugated sheet metal façade coated in off-white. The relief on the façade envelope creates soft interplays of light and shade, its soft focus entering into a relationship with the surrounding vegetation. On the ground floor, the fair-faced concrete base plate and plinth achieve a transition from the building to the garden.

The apartment buildings forming stages IV and V create an urban edge to Katzenbachpark in the north. They consist of a series of stereometrically related volumes that adapt to the different property depths and derive their appearance from their interior spatial requirements. Inside the apartments, the residential spatial figures develop between these polygonal exterior forms, the corner loggias facing south towards the park and the rectangular rooms. From the street, multiple views into the park are afforded through the buildings, opening and closing in the perception of passers-by. The dark façade cladding made of reddish brown varnished ceramic plates sets the buildings apart from the green of the park.

Projektwettbewerb mit Präqualifikation 2009, 1. Preis
Projekt: Ersatzneubauten mit 186 Wohnungen
Bauherr: Baugenossenschaft Glattal, Zürich
Ausführung: 2010–2013, 2015, 2019
Zusammenarbeit: Edelaar Mosayebi Inderbitzin Architekten (BS+EMI Architektenpartner), Zürich
Landschaftsarchitektur: Tremp Landschaftsarchitekten, Zürich

Project competition with prequalification, 2009, 1st Prize
Project: Replacement buildings for 186 apartments
Client: Baugenossenschaft Glattal, Zurich
Construction: 2010–2013, 2015, 2019
Collaboration: Edelaar Mosayebi Inderbitzin Architekten (BS+EMI Architektenpartner), Zurich
Landscape architecture: Tremp Landschaftsarchitekten, Zurich

Skizze Katzenbach III
Sketch, Katzenbach III

Verwaltungsgebäude Eternit in Glarus von Haefeli Moser Steiger, 1954–1955
Eternit administrative building in Glarus by Haefeli Moser Steiger, 1954–1955

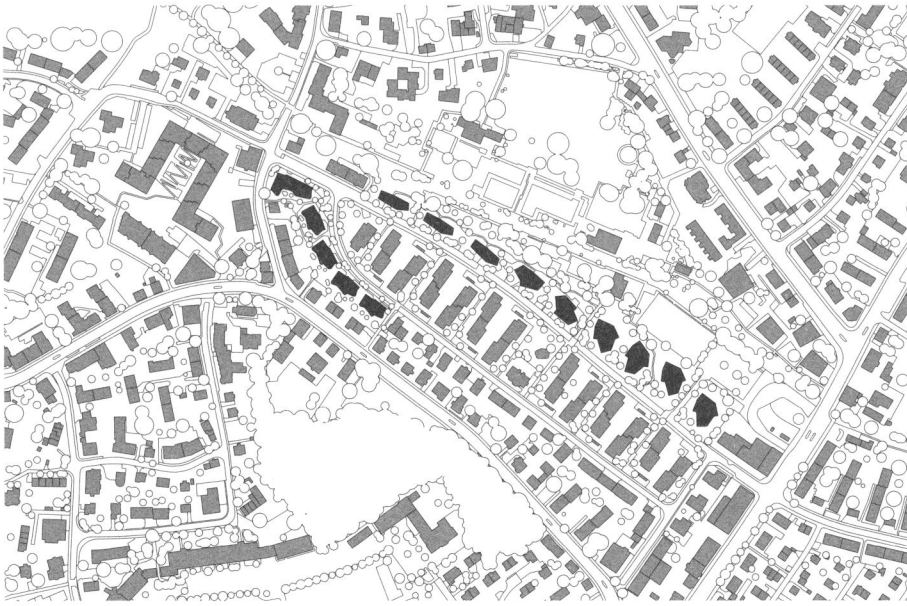

Situation 1:7500
Site plan **1:7500**

Katzenbach IV
Grundriss Regelgeschoss 1:800
Katzenbach IV
Standard floor plan 1:800

Katzenbach III
Grundriss Regelgeschoss 1:800
Katzenbach III
Standard floor plan 1:800

WOHNÜBERBAUUNG GUGGACH, ZÜRICH-UNTERSTRASS

GUGGACH RESIDENTIAL DEVELOPMENT, ZURICH UNTERSTRASS

Die Wohnüberbauung Guggach befindet sich an einer topografisch wie auch städtebaulich markanten Lage im Sattel von Zürichberg und Käferberg, an der Nahtstelle zwischen der Zürcher Innenstadt und Nordstadt. An dieser zentralen städtischen Lage entsteht eine neue urbane Verdichtung durch vier mehrgeschossige Apartmenthäuser. Sie umklammern das gesamte Areal in seiner Ausdehnung von Osten nach Westen. Das Projekt betont im architektonischen Ausdruck und in der Gestaltung des Aussenraums seinen urbanen Charakter.

Die mit dunklen Farben hinterlegten Gussglasfassaden vermitteln zum Hintergrund der ansteigenden Waldflanke, gleichzeitig zeigen sie in wechselnder Wirkung zwischen Schwere und Entmaterialisierung artifizielle Qualitäten. Der Aussenraum wird bestimmt durch grossflächige Wasserspiegel, die über Momente der Reflexion die Fassaden in die Aussenraumbildung miteinbeziehen.

Die Wohnungen bauen im Grundriss auf einer Kreuzfigur auf, welche die Nord-Süd-Orientierung der Gebäudekörper zu einer Allseitigkeit erweitern, sodass auch Morgen- und Abendlicht in die Wohnräume fällt. Über den Grundriss, die Fassadenwicklung und -materialisierung sowie die Aussenraumgestaltung entsteht ein hohes Mass an Kohärenz zwischen Städtebau, Wohnform und architektonischem Ausdruck.

The Guggach housing estate is situated at a striking location, both topographically and in terms of urban planning, on the saddle between the Zürichberg and Käferberg hills at the threshold between downtown Zurich and the northern part of the city. The central urban location achieves a new urban densification with four multi-storey apartment buildings. Their east-west expanse frames the entire area. The project's architectural expression and the design of the exterior grounds highlight the location's urban character.

The dark-coloured cast glass façades mediate with the background of the rising forest flank, while also staging an interplay between heavy and dematerialised artificial qualities. The exterior space is defined by large-scale water basins that reflect the façades and thereby involve them in characterising the area.

The apartments are basically cruciform, thereby extending the building's north-south orientation to achieve aspects on all sides. Even morning and evening sunlight enters into the apartments in this way. The floor plan, the façade development, its materialisation and the design of the exterior space all contribute to achieving a high level of coherence between urban planning, the residential form and the architectural expression.

Projektwettbewerb auf Einladung 2011, 1. Preis
Projekt: Wohnüberbauung mit 200 Eigentumswohnungen
Bauherr: Allreal Generalunternehmung AG, Zürich
Ausführung: 2011–2015
Zusammenarbeit: Edelaar Mosayebi Inderbitzin Architekten (BS+EMI Architektenpartner), Zürich
Landschaftsarchitektur: Blau und Gelb Landschaftsarchitekten, Rapperswil

Invitation project competition in 2011, 1st Prize
Project: Housing development with 200 owner-occupied apartments
Client: Allreal Generalunternehmung AG, Zurich
Construction: 2011–2015
Collaboration: Edelaar Mosayebi Inderbitzin Architekten (BS+EMI Architektenpartner), Zurich
Landscape architecture: Blau und Gelb Landschaftsarchitekten, Rapperswil

Wasserspiegel im Parkhof: Wohnsiedlung Point-du-Jour in Boulogne-Billancourt von Fernand Pouillon, 1957–1963
Fountain in a park courtyard: Point-du-Jour housing estate in Boulogne-Billancourt by Fernand Pouillon, 1957–1963

Gussglasfassade
Cast glass façade

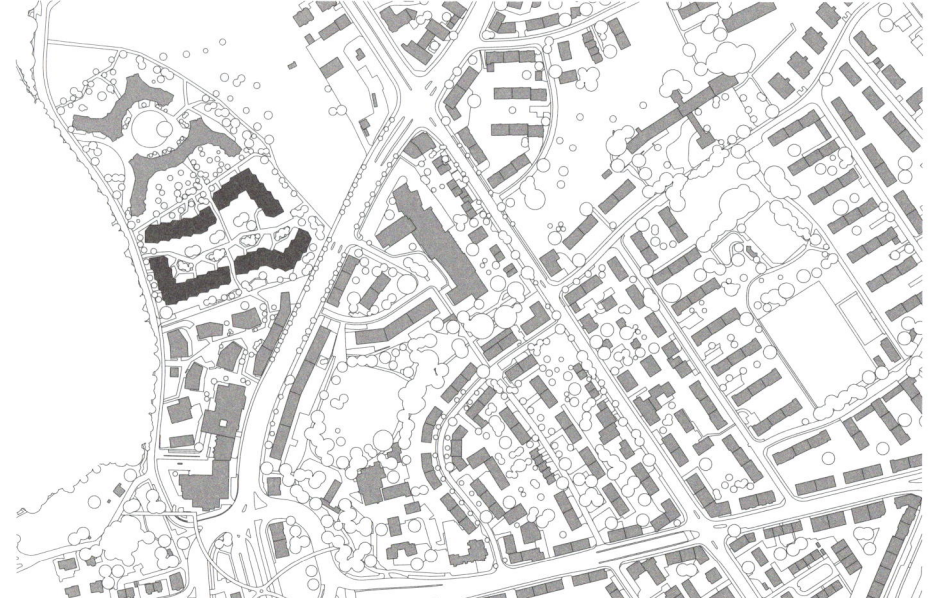

Situation 1:7500
Site plan 1:7500

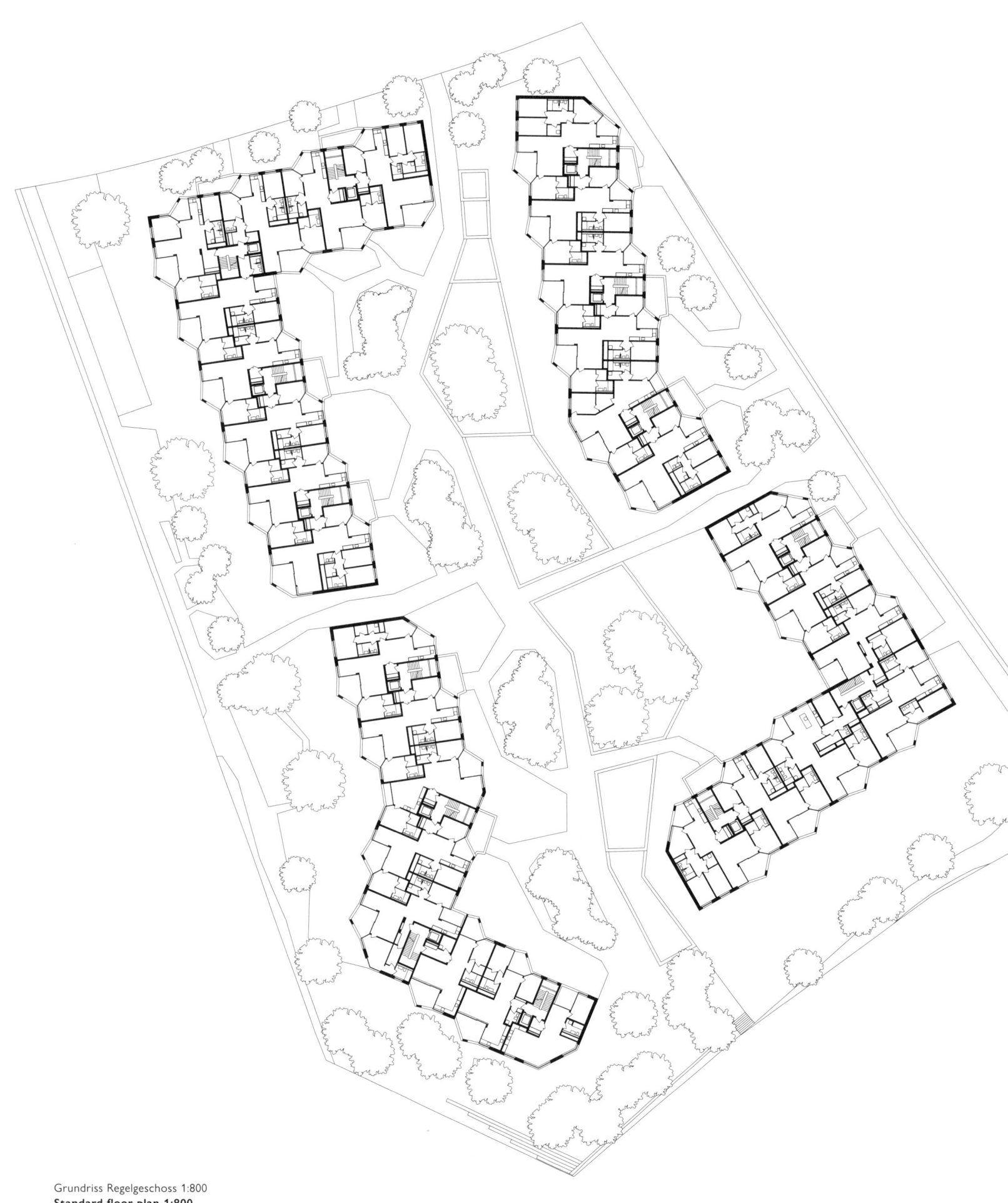

Grundriss Regelgeschoss 1:800
Standard floor plan 1:800

MULTIFUNKTIONALES WOHNHAUS, OETWIL AM SEE

MULTIFUNCTIONAL RESIDENTIAL BUILDING, OETWIL AM SEE

Der Neubau an der Bergstrasse bildet den Auftakt zu einer zukünftigen Wohnbebauung auf dem heutigen Landwirtschaftsareal des Schlösslihofs. Er ersetzt eine eindrückliche Scheune und schafft als Laubenhaus, das sich typologisch an ländlichen Vorbildern orientiert, dabei aber einen eigenständigen Ausdruck besitzt, eine neue Identität für die gesamte Parzelle.

Die Grundrissstruktur entstand ausgehend von dem Wunsch des Bauherrn, das Wohnhaus in den ersten Jahren als Provisorium für zwei psychiatrische Stationen zu nutzen. Es wurde daher eine nutzungsneutrale Kammerung gewählt, die ideal für Klinikstationen ist und zu einem späteren Zeitpunkt mit nur wenigen Eingriffen zu Wohnungen umgebaut werden kann. Der Wohnungstyp orientiert sich dabei an dem bäuerlichen Wohnen: Über die Laube tritt man direkt in eine grosse Wohnküche, über die alle weiteren Räume erschlossen werden.

Der Ausdruck des Hauses ist durch seine äussere Tragstruktur aus grün lasierten Betonstützen und eine Hülle aus auberginefarbenen sägerohen Brettern geprägt. Zusammen mit den aussen dunklen Holzmetallfenstern, welche die Raumtiefe der Lauben betonen, wird eine Homogenisierung der Materialien erreicht, die eine ruhige Eleganz ausstrahlt. Mit dem matten Rot des Holzkleids werden Erinnerungen an die Farbe der ehemaligen Scheune geweckt, mit seinen Grüntönen fügt sich das Haus in den Kontext der angrenzenden Obstwiesen ein.

The new development on Bergstrasse forms the beginning of a future residential estate on the former agriculturally used land known as the Schlösslihof. It replaces an impressive barn and creates a new identity for the entire plot as an arbour house, which is typologically based on rural models, but has its own independent expression.

The floor-plan structure was based on the client's wish to use the building in the first few years as temporary accommodation for two psychiatric wards. Thus, rooms were designed to have neutral uses, since this is ideal for clinic wards and allows them to be converted into apartments at a later date with only a few interventions. The housing type refers to agricultural living: from the arbour, one enters directly into a large combined kitchen and dining room, from where all other rooms are accessed.

The building's expression is characterised by its exterior load-bearing structure of green-painted concrete supports and an envelope of aubergine-coloured rough-sawn boards. Together with the dark wood-metal windows, which accentuate the arbours' spatial depth, this makes the materials homogeneous, radiating a peaceful elegance. The colour of the former barn is recalled in the matt red of the wooden cladding, while the building's green tone integrates it into the context of the neighbouring orchards.

Planerwahlverfahren 2013, 1. Preis
Projekt: Neubau, Wohnhaus mit 22 Wohnungen, temporäre Nutzung als Klinik für zwei psychiatrische Stationen
Bauherr: Hinderer Liegenschaften AG, Oetwil am See
Ausführung: 2014–2016

Planner-selection process in 2013, 1st Prize
Project: New development of a residential building with 22 apartments, temporary use as a clinic for two psychiatric wards
Client: Hinderer Liegenschaften AG, Oetwil am See
Construction: 2014–2016

Umbau ehemalige Hoteldependance, Walenstadtberg, Peter Märkli, 1992
Conversion of the former hotel annexe, Walenstadtberg, Peter Märkli, 1992

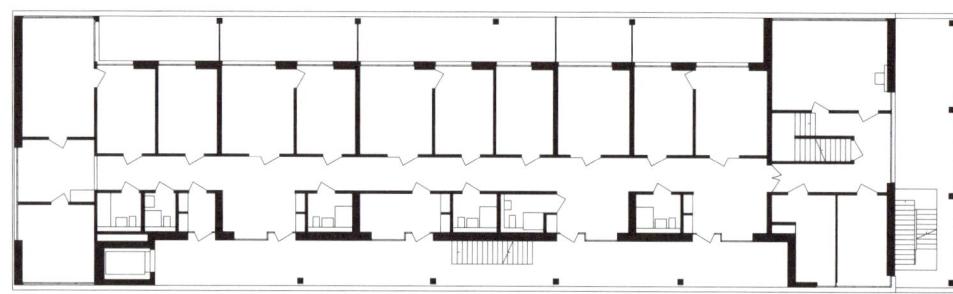

Grundriss Regelgeschoss für Kliniknutzung 1:400
Standard floor plan for clinic use 1:400

WOHNSIEDLUNG TOBLERSTRASSE, ZÜRICH-FLUNTERN

TOBLERSTRASSE HOUSING ESTATE, ZURICH FLUNTERN

Das Quartier Fluntern ist durch eine homogene städtebauliche Körnung von «Punktbauten in Gärten» geprägt, die über eine repräsentative Gestalt und strassenseitige Eingänge verfügen. Ausgehend davon wurden dreizehn kompakte Solitärbauten mit eindeutiger Strassenfassade realisiert, die trotz deutlich höherer Bebauungsdichte typologisch und stimmungsmässig an den Bestand anknüpfen.

Durch Drehen und Spiegeln der im Wesentlichen gleichen Häuser wird der Ausdruck von repetitiven, schematischen Baukörpern vermieden. Vielmehr entsteht eine Komposition aus unterschiedlichen, sich geradezu organisch aufeinander beziehenden Volumina mit kabinettartigen Aussenräumen im Inneren der Siedlung. Das Knicken der Fassaden erzeugt quartiersübliche Fassadenlängen und spielt die eigentliche Grösse der Volumina herunter. Das Ergebnis ist ein formbildendes Gleichgewicht zwischen Bauvolumen und Aussenraum.

Die Wohnungen entwickeln sich als Raumkontinuum um einen zentralen Kern mit Nasszellen und einer zum Wohnen hin offenen Küche. Durch die Vermeidung von Korridoren entstehen geräumige, unterschiedlich möblierbare Wohnräume und grosszügige Eingangsbereiche. Vielseitige Erschliessungs- und Zirkulationsmöglichkeiten vermitteln trotz knapp bemessener Fläche den Eindruck einer räumlichen Grosszügigkeit.

Die Häuser setzen im Ausdruck die Homogenität des Quartiers fort und verleihen der Siedlung zugleich eine eigene Identität. Einerseits werden daher bestehende Motive und Stimmungen aufgenommen und zu einem neuen, eigenständigen Ausdruck verdichtet. Andererseits wird das städtebauliche Thema der frei stehenden Einzelhäuser mit kabinettartigen Gartenräumen reflektiert und verfeinert.

The Fluntern neighbourhood is characterised by a homogenous urban-planning grain of free-standing buildings in gardens, which have a prestigious appearance and entrances facing the street side. From that initial situation, thirteen compact free-standing buildings were built with a clear street-facing façade. Despite their significantly higher development density, they still pick up on the typology and atmosphere of the existing development.

The expression of repetitive, schematic buildings can be avoided by rotating and reflecting the basically similar buildings. This creates a composition consisting of different volumes that essentially refer to each other organically, with cabinet-like exterior spaces inside the estate. Folded façades adhere to the common lengths and underplay the actual size of the volumes. The result is a formally organising balance between the building volume and the exterior space.

The apartments develop out of the spatial continuum around a central core, with sanitary units and a kitchen that opens out towards the living area. Avoiding corridors creates spacious living areas that can be variably furnished, as well as generous entrance halls. Diverse access and circulation possibilities give the impression of spaciousness despite the limited area.

The buildings' expression picks up on the homogeneity of the neighbourhood and also gives the estate an identity. This continues the existing motifs and atmospheres, concentrating them to create an autonomous expression. Furthermore, the urban planning theme of free-standing individual houses with cabinet-like gardens is reflected upon and refined.

Projektwettbewerb mit Präqualifikation 2010, 1. Preis
Projekt: Ersatzneubauten mit 170 Wohnungen
Bauherr: Allgemeine Baugenossenschaft Zürich, Zürich
Ausführung: 2011–2017
Zusammenarbeit: Edelaar Mosayebi Inderbitzin Architekten (BS+EMI Architektenpartner), Zürich
Landschaftsarchitektur: Lorenz Eugster Landschaftsarchitektur und Städtebau, Zürich

Project competition with prequalification in 2010, 1st Prize
Project: Replacement buildings with 170 apartments
Client: Allgemeine Baugenossenschaft Zürich
Construction: 2011–2017
Collaboration: Edelaar Mosayebi Inderbitzin Architekten (BS+EMI Architektenpartner), Zurich
Landscape architecture: Lorenz Eugster Landschaftsarchitektur und Städtebau, Zurich

Wohnhaus Girasol in Madrid von José Antonio Coderch, 1966
Girasol residential building in Madrid by José Antonio Coderch, 1966

Wohnbauten an der Toblerstrasse
Residential buildings along Toblerstrasse

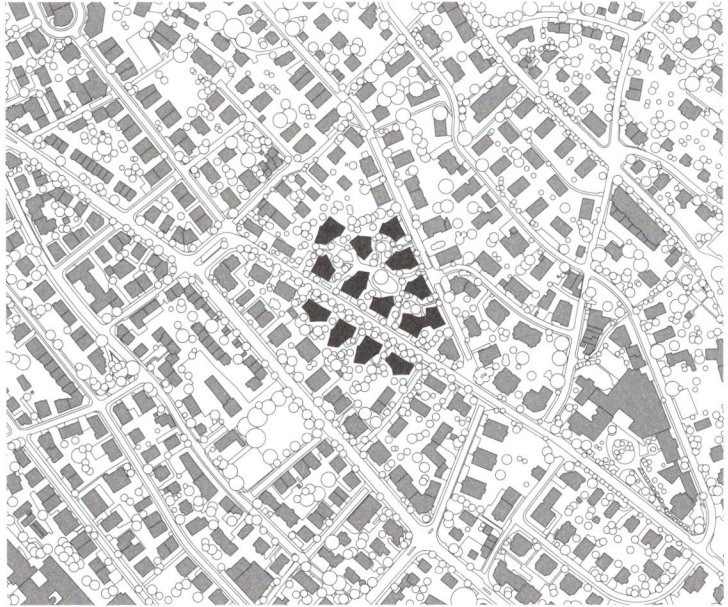

Situation 1:7500
Site plan 1:7500

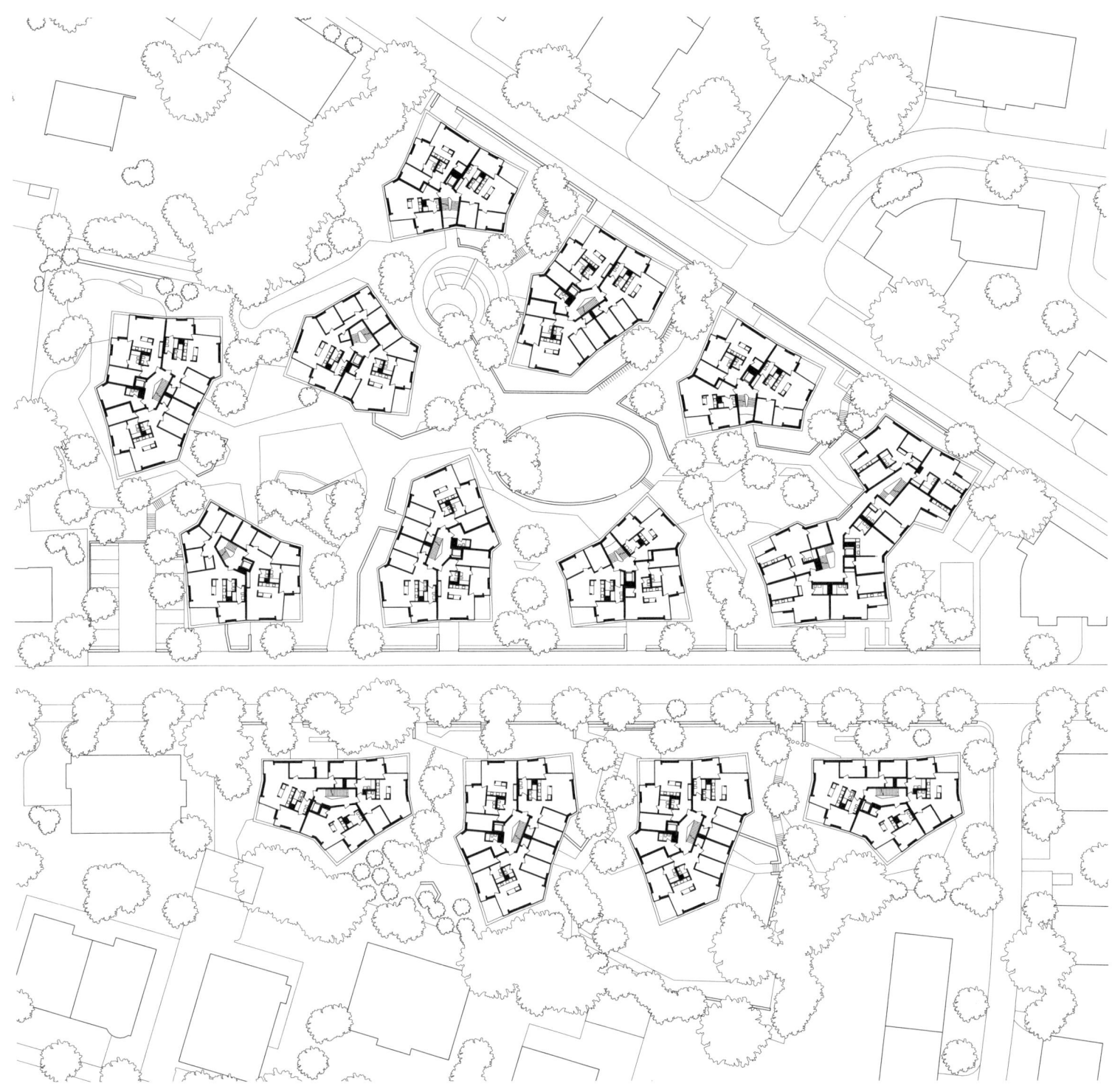

Grundriss Regelgeschoss 1:1000
Standard floor plan 1:1000

MEHRFAMILIENHAUS OTTIKERSTRASSE, ZÜRICH

APARTMENT BUILDING OTTIKERSTRASSE, ZURICH

Die Parzelle an der Ottikerstrasse liegt an der Grenze der Quartiere Ober- und Unterstrass. Am Ende des 19. Jahrhunderts wurde dieses Gebiet mit einer bürgerlich-repräsentativen Architektur bebaut, wie sie in Zürich nur selten zu finden ist. An der Ottikerstrasse selbst manifestiert die eklektizistische Architektur des Fin de Siècle ihren Höhepunkt.

Das neue Haus setzt sich mit diesem reichhaltigen architektonischen Erbe auseinander. Basierend auf dem ursprünglichen Bebauungsplan aus dem 19. Jahrhundert besetzt es den Baulinien folgend markant die Strassenkreuzung. Durch die plastisch-expressiv gegliederte Fassade mit einer ausgeprägten Vertikalen und einer volumetrischen Betonung an der Kreuzung werden architektonische Elemente der umliegenden Häuser aufgenommen. Das Haus mit seinem betonten Dachabschluss wirkt turmartig und nimmt Bezug auf das architektonische Repertoire des Kontexts. Die Seitenfassaden und die Gartenfassade sind deutlich einfacher formuliert.

Den benachbarten Häusern entsprechend liegt der Hauseingang im Hochparterre an der nördlichen Seitenfassade. Über eine Eingangshalle und ein innen liegendes Treppenhaus werden pro Geschoss zwei grosse Wohnungen erschlossen. Die Grundrisse der Wohnungen orientieren sich ebenso an den gekammerten Raumabfolgen des 19. Jahrhunderts wie an Elementen moderner Wohnformen.

Die sorgfältige Detaillierung und eine haptisch hochwertige Materialisierung verankern das Haus in seinem Kontext.

The plot on Ottikerstrasse is situated on the boundary between the Oberstrass and Unterstrass neighbourhoods. At the end of the 19th century, the area was developed with bourgeois, prestigious architecture that is rare elsewhere in Zurich. The eclectic *fin de siècle* architecture experienced its climax along Ottikerstrasse itself.

The new building addresses that diverse architectural heritage. Based on the original development plan from the 19th century, it strikingly occupies the street junction, following the original building lines. The architectural elements of the surrounding buildings are picked up on through the sculptural, expressively structured façade with striking vertical and volumetric accentuation at the junction. The building, with its prominent roof conclusion, has a tower-like quality, thereby referring to the architectural repertoire of the context. The side and garden façades are formulated in a much simpler way.

In accordance with the neighbouring buildings, the house entrance is on the mezzanine level on the northern façade. Two apartments per floor are accessed via an entrance hall and an interior staircase. The apartment floor plans are orientated towards 19th-century chambered spatial sequences, as well as modern forms of living.

The careful detailing and high-quality, haptic materials anchor the building in its context.

Direktauftrag 2014
Projekt: Wohnhaus mit 10 Wohnungen und Gewerbeflächen
Bauherr: privat
Ausführung: 2016–2018

Direct contract in 2014
Project: Residential building with 10 apartments and commercial spaces
Client: private
Construction: 2016–2018

Mehrfamilienhaus an der Ottikerstrasse von Stieger & Cie, 1905
Apartment building in Ottikerstrasse by Stieger & Cie, 1905

Wohnhaus an der Via Quadronno von Angelo Mangiarotti in Mailand, 1962
Residential building on Via Quadronno in Milan, by Angelo Mangiarotti, 1962

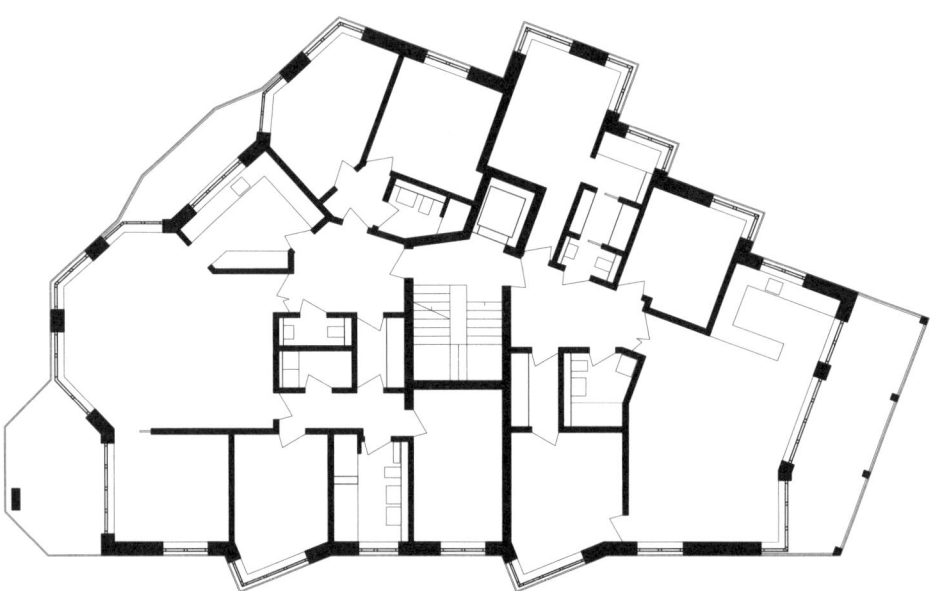

Grundriss Regelgeschoss 1:250
Standard floor plan 1:250

WOHNÜBERBAUUNG AM CHATZEBACH, MURI

AM CHATZEBACH HOUSING DEVELOPMENT, MURI

Prägend für die Gemeinde Muri ist die Klosteranlage, von der aus Strassen, Wege und Gebäudestrukturen strahlenförmig in den Landschaftsraum führen. Ähnlich den vorhandenen Häusern aus dem 19. Jahrhundert und den Ökonomiegebäuden um das Kloster sind die Wohnhäuser am Williweg als «Häuser im Garten» konzipiert. Aufgrund ihrer Nähe zueinander entsteht der Eindruck eines strassenbegleitenden Gesamtbaukörpers, der volumetrisch an das lang gezogene Klostergebäude erinnert und die zum Kloster führende Strasse in ihrer Ausrichtung betont. Über die Staffelung der Volumina entstehen schmale Zwischenräume, welche Durchblicke in die Gärten freigeben. Entgegen den strengen Strassenfassaden besitzen die dreigeschossigen Wohnhäuser gartenseitig eine durchlässige Laubenschicht. Zweigeschossige Gartenhäuser ergänzen das Wohnangebot und bilden den Übergang zum angrenzenden Einfamilienhausquartier.

Bis auf einen Dreispänner sind alle Häuser als Zweispänner erschlossen. Dies ermöglicht eine dreiseitige Belichtung der Wohnungen und die Orientierung der Wohnräume sowohl zum Garten als auch zu den Ankunftshöfen am Williweg. Die öffentlicheren Wohnfunktionen wie Küche, Ess- und Wohnraum sind bei den direkt an der Strasse liegenden Häusern diagonal aufgebaut. Bei den zurückspringenden Häusern ist die Wohnraumfigur linear angeordnet.

Gemäss ihrer städtebaulichen Haltung als strassenbegleitende, stattliche Häuser am Übergang zu den Gärten weisen die Häuser zum Garten und zur Zugangsseite je unterschiedliche Fassaden auf und suchen über ein hölzernes dunkelgrünes Kleid zugleich eine städtische Eleganz wie auch die Nähe zum Garten.

The local monastery complex in Muri is the community's definitive characteristic, from where the roads, paths and building structures radiate into the landscape. Like the existing 19th-century houses and the auxiliary buildings around the monastery, the houses along Williweg are conceived as "houses in the gardens". Their mutual proximity creates the impression of a street-accompanying structure that recalls the volumetrics of the elongated monastery and strengthens the orientation of the street leading to the monastery. The buildings' placement is staggered, creating narrow interstices that allow views into the gardens. Unlike the strict street façade, the three-storey apartment buildings have a permeable arbour layer on the garden side. Two-storey garden houses complement the housing offer and form a transition to the adjoining neighbourhood of single-family homes.

Apart from one building with three apartments per floor, the others have two apartments per floor. This enables natural lighting for the apartments on three sides and aspects towards both the garden and the arrival courtyards along Williweg. The less private residential functions such as the kitchen, dining room and living room have a diagonal arrangement in the buildings situated directly along the street. The living-room figures in the houses that recede away from the street have a more linear arrangement.

In accordance with the project's urban planning approach as stately homes that line the street, different façades are used at the transition to the garden and the access side. They use dark green, wooden cladding that expresses urban elegance as well as the garden's proximity.

Studienauftrag auf Einladung 2016, 1. Preis
Projekt: Neubauten mit 55 Wohnungen
Bauherr: Genossenschaft für Wohnkultur, Muri
Ausführung 2017–2019
Zusammenarbeit: Stücheli, Pestalozzi, Schiratzki Architekten, Zürich

Invitation contracted study in 2016, 1st Prize
Project: New buildings with 55 apartments
Client: Genossenschaft für Wohnkultur, Muri
Construction: 2017–2019
Collaboration: Stücheli, Pestalozzi, Schiratzki Architekten, Zurich

Pfarrhaus in Ziefen, 1841
Rectory in Ziefen, 1841

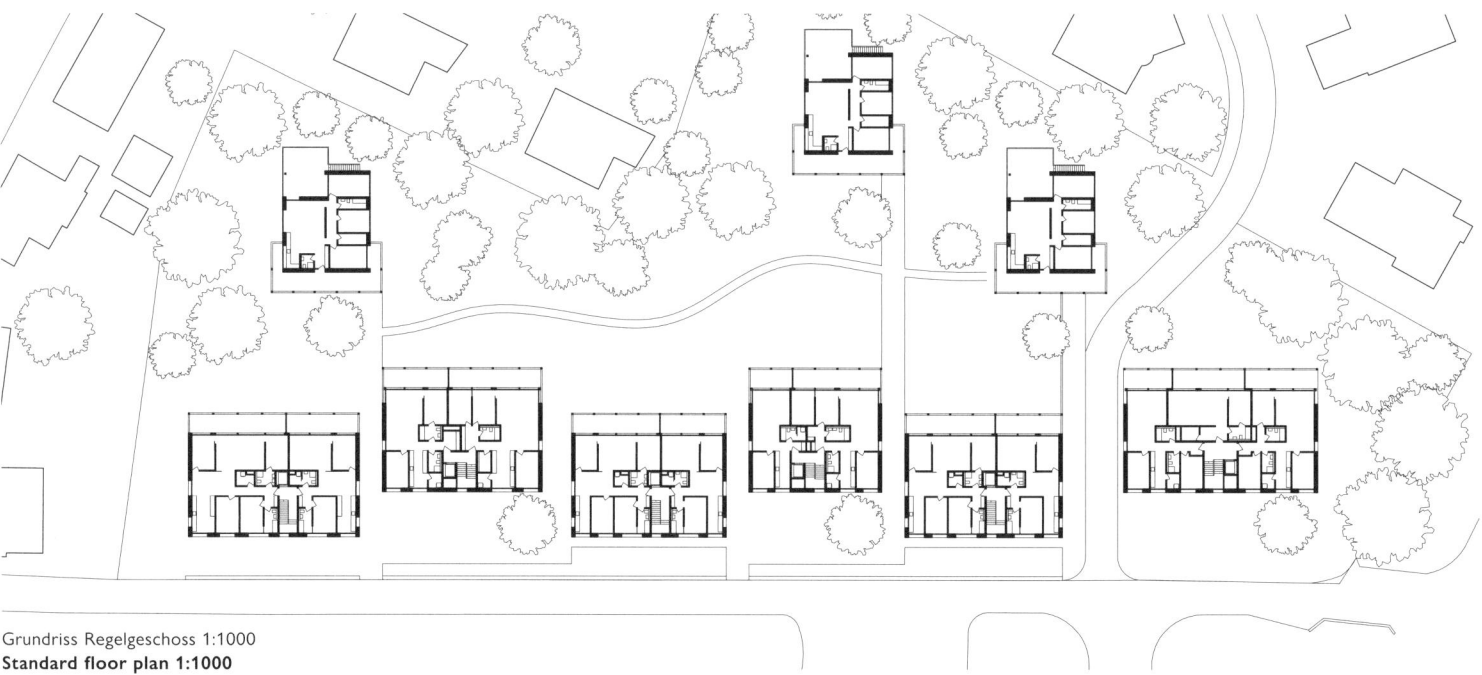

Grundriss Regelgeschoss 1:1000
Standard floor plan 1:1000

LOKSTADT, WINTERTHUR

Auf dem ehemaligen Industrieareal Werk 1 im Sulzerareal entsteht ein neues Quartier mit Wohn- und Gewerbenutzung, dessen historische Identität durch ein subtiles Weiterbauen erhalten werden soll.

Den Auftakt bilden die Wohnüberbauungen auf den Baufeldern 3 und 5. Die Zeile auf Baufeld 5, ein ehemaliges Portalgebäude, zählt zu den ältesten Bauten auf dem Areal und ist über ihre Permanenz identitätsstiftend. Vorgesehen sind unterschiedliche Wohn- und Arbeitsmodelle. Die für industrielle Bauten idealtypischen Gebäudestrukturen weisen dafür die nötige Flexibilität auf, weshalb ein Teil des Bestands erhalten und transformiert wird. Im Ausdruck weisen die Stadthäuser Referenzen an die industriellen Bestandsbauten auf.

Im neuen Hofhaus auf Baufeld 3 sind verschiedene Wohneinheiten vorgesehen: zum neuen Dialogplatz orientierte Eigentumswohnungen, genossenschaftliche Familienwohnungen an der kopfartig ausgebildeten Nordwestseite, Alterswohnungen an der Südwestseite und Kleinwohnungen mit dreiseitiger Ausrichtung in Südlage. Gefasst werden die Einheiten durch einen klaren volumetrischen Zuschnitt mit einer feinen mehrfachen Übergiebelung, wie man sie von grossflächigen Industriehallen kennt. In seiner volumetrischen Gliederung, dem gewählten architektonischen Vokabular und der strukturellen Ordnung als Holzbau bezieht sich das Hofhaus auf die umliegenden Hallenbauten, besitzt zugleich jedoch eine eigene Identität.

On the former industrial site Werk 1 in the Sulzerareal in Winterthur, a new neighbourhood with residential and commercial uses is being developed in a way that preserves its historical identity through subtle continued construction.

The first developments will be housing on plots 3 and 5. The row on plot 5, a former portal building, is among the oldest structures on the site and strengthens its identity with its permanence. Different residential and working models are planned. The typical industrial building structures have the necessary flexibility, which is why part of the existing structures were preserved and transformed. The expression of the townhouses refers to the existing industrial buildings.

Various housing units are planned for the new courtyard house on plot 3: owner-occupied apartments facing the new Dialogplatz, housing corporation apartments for families at the northwestern side, which is developed into a head end, housing for the elderly on the southwestern side and small apartments with a three-sided orientation located to the south. The units are framed by a clear volumetric delineation, including fine multiple gabling, as is familiar in large-scale industrial halls. The volumetric structure, the chosen architectural vocabulary and the structural order as a wooden building are all ways in which the courtyard house refers to the surrounding industrial buildings, while retaining its own identity.

Wettbewerb mit Präqualifikation 2016, 1. Preis
Projekt: Neubauten mit Gewerbeflächen und 300 Wohnungen
Bauherr: Implenia Schweiz, Dietlikon
Ausführung: 2018–2021
Zusammenarbeit: KilgaPopp Architekten, Winterthur
Landschaftsarchitektur: Hager Partner, Zürich

Competition with prequalification in 2016, 1st Prize
Project: New buildings with commercial spaces and 300 apartments
Client: Implenia Schweiz
Construction: 2018–2021
Collaboration: KilgaPopp Architekten, Winterthur
Landscape architecture: Hager Partner, Zurich

Ehemalige Werkhalle mit Kopfbau und Aufsatz, Baufeld 3
Former factory workshop with frontage building and top section, Building site 3

Ehemalige Industriehalle auf dem Sulzerareal
Former industrial hall, Sulzerareal

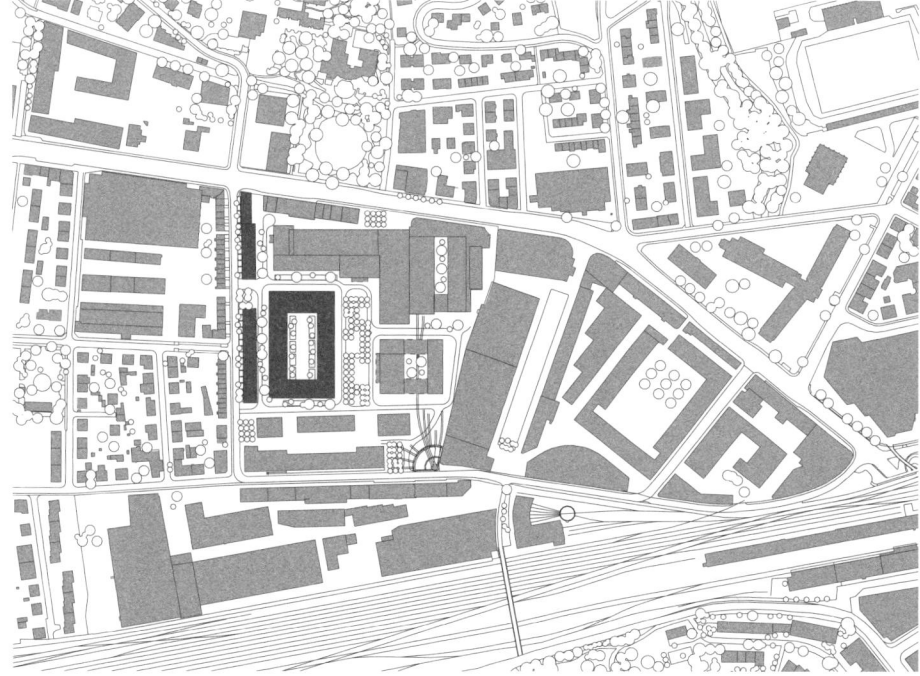

Situation 1:7500
Site plan 1:7500

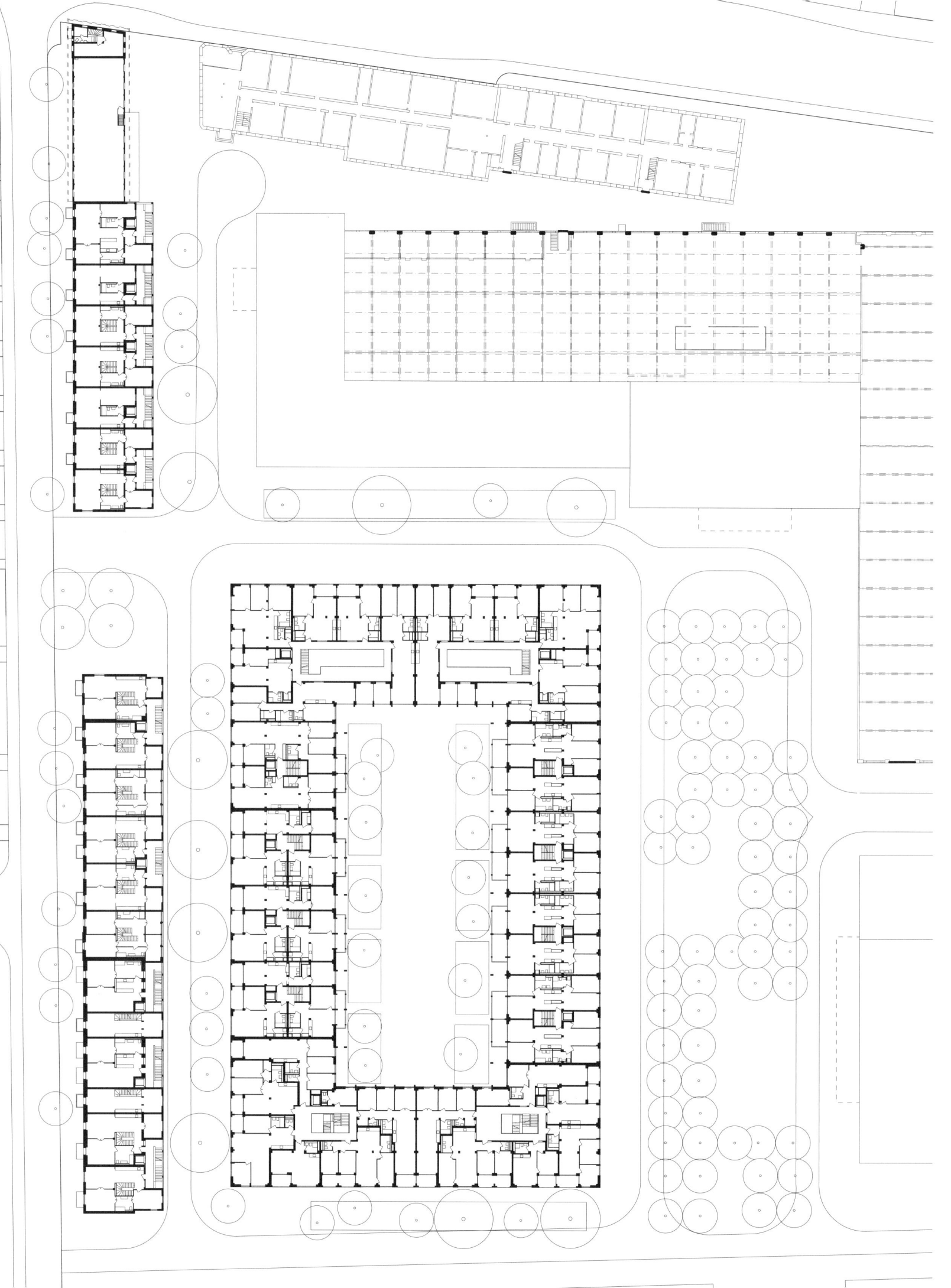

Grundriss Regelgeschoss 1:800
Standard floor plan 1:800

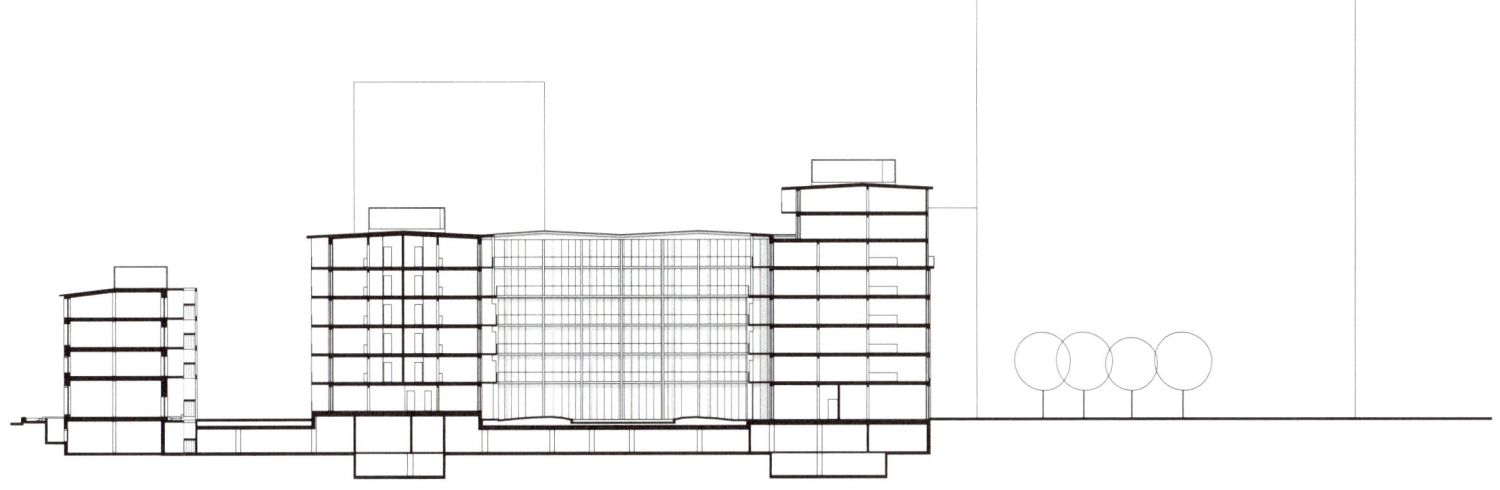

Querschnitt 1:800
Sectional view 1:800

WOHNSIEDLUNG SCHWAMENDINGER-DREIECK, ZÜRICH-SCHWAMENDINGEN

SCHWAMENDINGER-DREIECK HOUSING ESTATE, ZURICH SCHWAMENDINGEN

Der von Albert Heinrich Steiner um 1948 als Gartenstadt entworfene Stadtteil Schwamendingen besitzt noch heute seine Gültigkeit und hat viel von seinem ursprünglichen Charakter als Zürichs «Gartenzimmer» behalten. Der Entwurf adaptiert den Zeilenbautyp formal neu. Die charakteristische Zeilenform reagiert über Enge und Weite im Aussenraum sowie in der Perspektive verkürzte Baukörper auf die höhere Dichte. In der egalitären Behandlung von Orientierung, Aussenraum und Strassenbezug sowie in der allseitigen Vernetzung und Durchwegung knüpft das Projekt an die Qualitäten des Steiner-Plans an. Das Projekt sieht sechs s-förmig geschwungene Zeilen, jeweils gespiegelt und paarweise gruppiert, vor, die das gesamte Baufeld aufspannen. Zusammen mit den leichten Versätzen in den Bauzeilen erhalten die Bauten eine elegante, fein modulierte Gestalt. Eingeschossige Gewerbebauten an der Dübendorfstrasse verorten den Zeilenkopf zur Strasse hin.

Der vorgeschlagene Wohnungstyp mit der abtrennbaren Wohnküche ist aus der städtebaulichen Setzung entwickelt und unterstreicht die Schlankheit der Gebäudezeilen. Er vereint die Qualitäten des «Durchwohnens» mit den praktischen Vorzügen einer abschliessbaren Küche. Das Wohnzimmer mit den Balkonen liegt jeweils, alternierend in jeder Zeile, auf der Seite des weiteren Aussenraums. Die Hauszugänge befinden sich an der Stirnseite und in der Mitte der Zeile. Die geringfügigen Versätze in den Fassaden ermöglichen jeder Wohnung neben der primären Ost- und Westorientierung auch einen Blick nach Norden und Süden in die Tiefe des Aussenraums und zu den angrenzenden Baufeldern.

The district of Schwamendingen, which was planned as a garden city by A. H. Steiner around 1948, still has its relevance today and retains much of its original character as Zurich's "garden room". The design formally adapts the rowed housing type in a new way. The characteristic housing rows react to the narrow and broad exterior elements, as well as to the higher density through volumes that shorten when regarded in perspective. The project's egalitarian treatment of orientation, exterior spaces and the walkways picks up on the qualities of Steiner's original plan. The project plans six S-shaped rows, grouped in mirroring pairs, covering the entire building site. Together with the slightly staggered rows, the buildings gain an elegant, finely modulated appearance. Single-storey commercial buildings on Dübendorfstrasse locate the row's head end at the street.

The proposed living type with a detachable kitchen was developed out of the urban planning placement and highlights the slim nature of the building rows. It unites the qualities of open-plan living with the practical advantages of a kitchen that can be closed. The living room and its balconies are situated on the side of the additional exterior space, alternating its position in each housing row. The building entrances are at the head end and in the middle of the rows. The slightly staggered placement of the façades allows each apartment not only to have a primary east-west view, but also a north-south perspective, looking into the depth of the exterior space and towards the adjoining building sites.

Projektwettbewerb mit Präqualifikation 2014, 1. Preis
Projekt: Ersatzneubauten mit 233 Wohnungen
Bauherr: Baugenossenschaft Glattal, Zürich
Ausführung: 2017–2023
Zusammenarbeit: Edelaar Mosayebi Inderbitzin Architekten (BS+EMI Architektenpartner), Zürich
Landschaftsarchitektur: Hoffmann & Müller Landschaftsarchitektur, Zürich

Contract: Project competition with prequalification in 2014, 1st Prize
Project: Replacement building with 233 apartments
Client: Baugenossenschaft Glattal, Zurich
Construction: 2017–2023
Collaboration: Edelaar Mosayebi Inderbitzin Architekten (BS+EMI Architektenpartner), Zurich
Landscape architecture: Hoffmann & Müller Landschaftsarchitektur, Zurich

Wohnungsgrundriss 1:400
Apartment floor plan 1:400

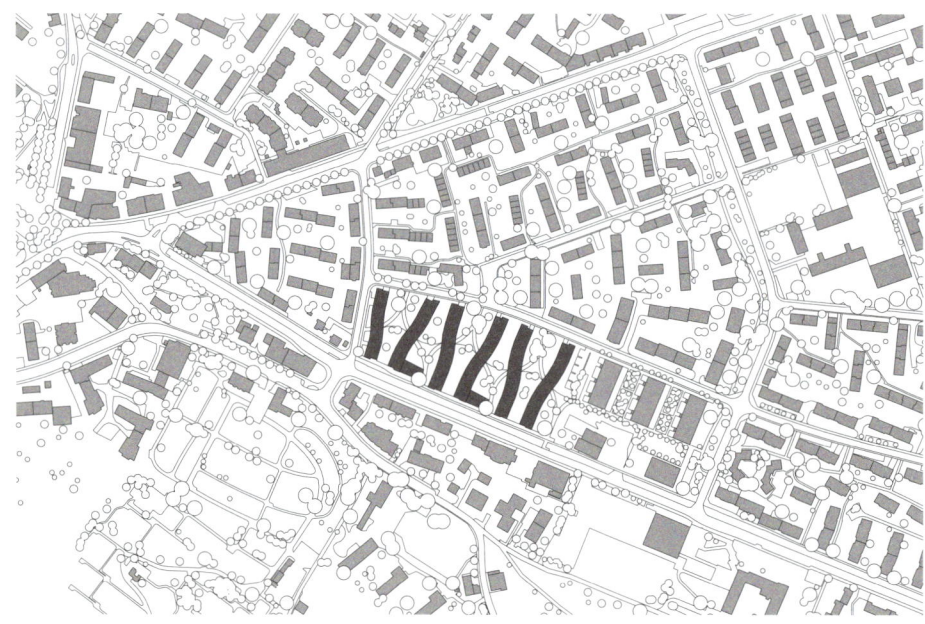

Situation 1:7500
Site plan 1:7500

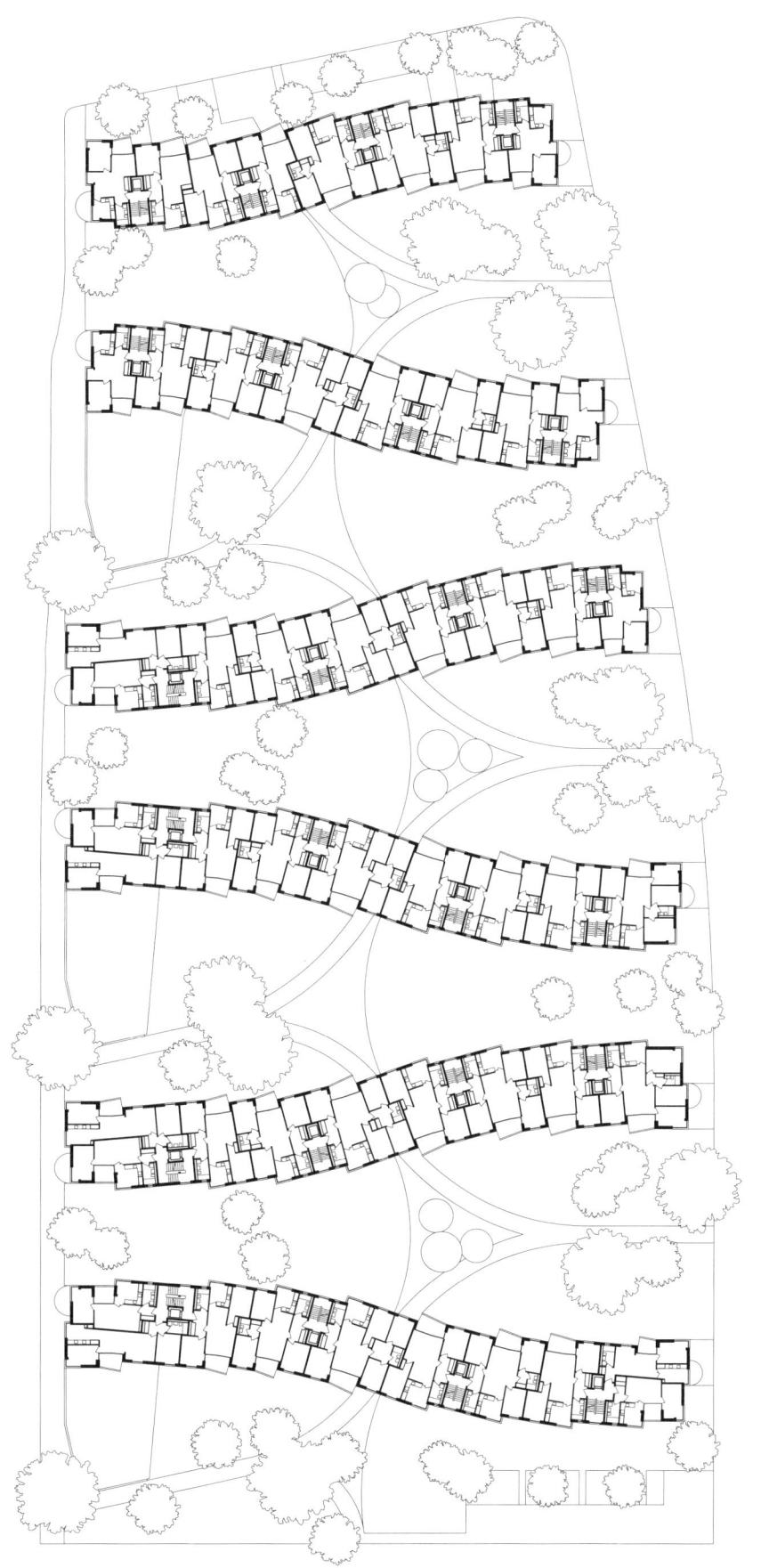

Grundriss Regelgeschoss 1:1000
Standard floor plan 1:1000

FELDMÜHLEAREAL, RORSCHACH

Rorschach besass in seinen Anfängen die Form eines Strassendorfs, das sich entlang des Bodenseeufers erstreckte. Im 19. Jahrhundert erfolgte eine ringartige Erweiterung mit einer orthogonalen Bebauungsstruktur, ausserhalb derer Ende des 19. Jahrhunderts grosse Gewerbe- und Industrieareale entstanden. Eins davon ist das Feldmühleareal, dessen Bestandsbauten diese Orthogonalität über die Bahntrasse hinaus fortsetzen. Aufgrund verschiedener Nutzungen und der damit einhergehenden Transformationen weist es heute eine für Industrieareale typische additive Hallenstruktur auf.

Das Areal soll unter Einbeziehung vorhandener Strukturen und Eigenheiten weithin als Ganzes erhalten bleiben. Die Grundorientierung bilden zwei bestehende, wichtige Sichtachsen, die das Areal als Gassen in Ost-West-Richtung gliedern. Entsprechend dem Bestand und der Gassen sind auch die Neubauten orthogonal ausgerichtet. Jeder Haustyp ist dabei durch eine aus der Nutzung entwickelte Typologie geprägt und besitzt seinen eigenen Charakter. Bis auf zwei Punktbauten greifen die Volumina die Höhe der vorhandenen Halle auf und bilden ein homogenes Gefüge unterschiedlicher Haustypen. Eine eigenständige Durchgrünung, die sich ausgehend vom angrenzenden Kirchenareal und dem Bach durch das gesamte Quartier bis zum Bahnhofplatz zieht, stärkt die Haltung, das Feldmühleareal als Ganzes zu lesen.

Initially, Rorschach was a linear settlement stretching along the shore of Lake Constance. In the 19th century, a ring-shaped development with an orthogonal building structure was added, outside of which major commercial and industrial grounds were established in the late 19th century. One of them is the Feldmühleareal. Its existing buildings continue the orthogonal structure beyond the railway line. Due to various uses and according conversions, it now has an additive hall structure that is typical of industrial estates.

It is planned that the estate should remain largely preserved with its existing structures and characteristics. The basic orientation is defined by two existing, important visual axes that structure the entire estate as walkways in an east-west direction. In accordance with the existing structures and walkways, the new buildings also have an orthogonal alignment. Each building type is characterised by a typology derived from its use and has its own character. Apart from two free-standing buildings, the volumes assume the height of the existing hall and create a homogenous structure of different building types. Autonomous greenery stretching from the adjoining church grounds through the entire neighbourhood and up to the station square consolidates the perspective of reading the Feldmühleareal as a unity.

Studienauftrag auf Einladung 2018, 1. Preis
Projekt: Neu- und Umbauten mit 300 Wohnungen und Gewerbeflächen
Bauherr: Steiner Investment Foundation AG, Zürich
Ausführung: 2021–2025
Landschaftsarchitektur: Hoffmann & Müller Landschaftsarchitektur, Zürich

Invitation contracted study in 2018, 1st Prize
Project: New buildings and conversions with 300 apartments and commercial units
Client: Steiner Investment Foundation AG, Zurich
Construction: 2021–2025
Landscape architecture: Hoffmann & Müller Landschaftsarchitektur, Zurich

Feldmühleareal, 1916

Wichtige Sichtachse zum angrenzenden Kirchenareal
Important visual axis to the church grounds

Schwarzplan Rorschach
Figure-ground diagram, Rorschach

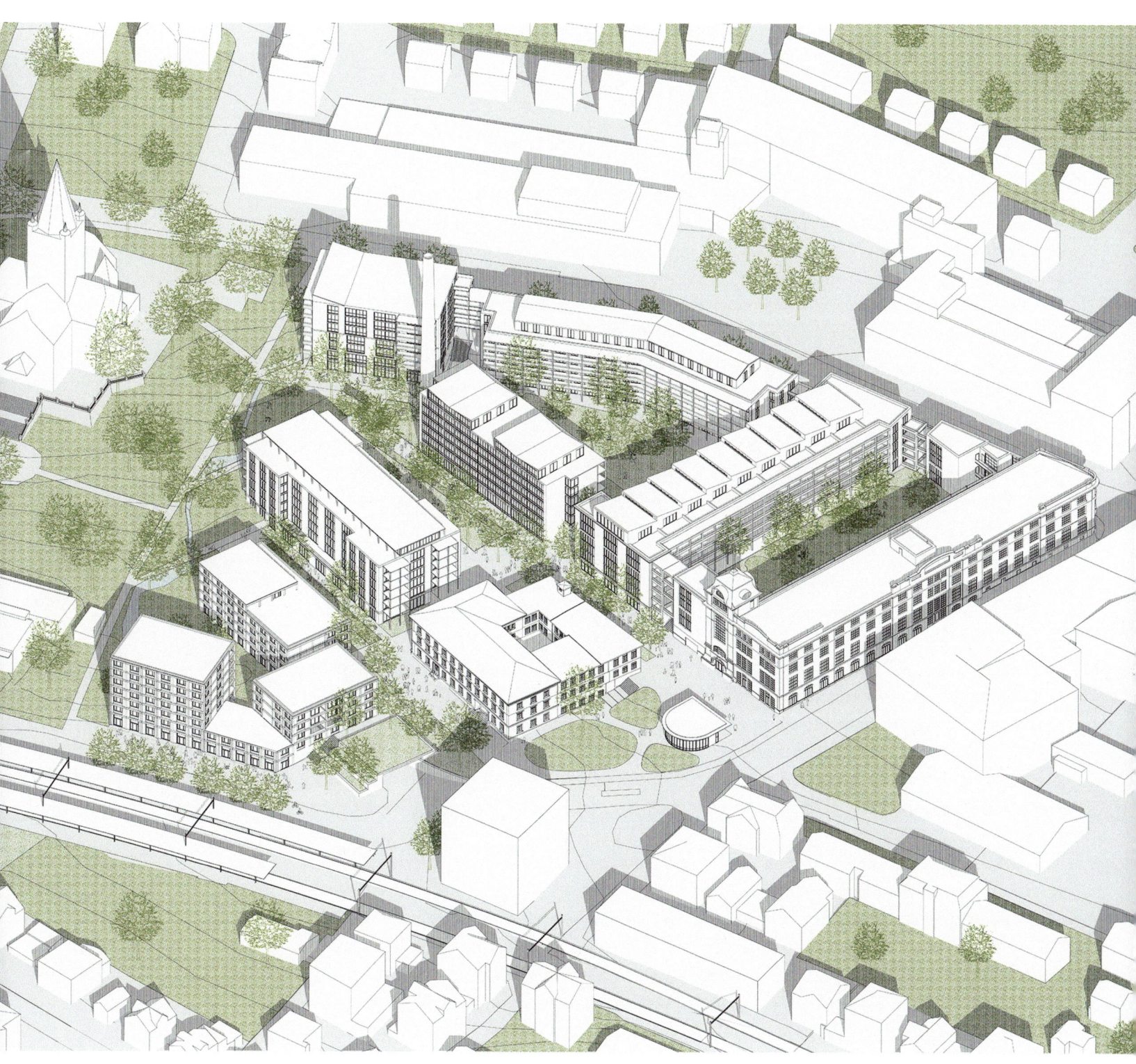

DIE WAHRNEHMUNG IM GEBRAUCH
UND DER GEBRAUCH DER WAHRNEHMUNG

Christoph Baumberger

Still und hell ist die Welt hinter Glas: zwischen den schon herbstlichen Bäumen das Mosaik der Häuser am gegenüberliegenden Ufer des Sees, über dem waldigen Hügelrücken ein so zarter wie unermesslicher Himmel, der verblasst gegen den Horizont, hinter dem sich die Gedanken im Unbestimmten verlieren. Zischend trappelt die Moka, als würde ein fernes Reiterheer über den Hügelrücken galoppieren. Einen Moment noch verweile ich in der nachmittäglichen Sonnenwärme am breiten Fenster des laubenartigen Schlafzimmers und folge dann dem Geruch des Kaffees. In der Küche ist es kühl und dämmrig. Die Handgriffe sind eingespielt, mein Körper weiss um die Anordnung von Herd, Schrank und Spüle, sodass ich während der Verrichtungen in Gedanken verbleiben kann. Mit der Mokkatasse in der Hand mache ich mich auf zum Arbeitszimmer. Nach der Küche die Enge des Office.

Dann wird es licht und weit um mich. Mit gesenktem Blick weiche ich Spielsachen aus, ehe das Wohnzimmer mich aufrechter gehen lässt. Im Spiegel über dem Kamin glitzert der See, wie ein heller Vogel schiesst ein Lichtreflex durch den Raum. Für einen Augenblick bin ich am Herbstmeer. Vertraut knarzt die Schwelle zum Arbeitszimmer, wo mich erneut Dämmer umfängt. Durch das offene Fenster strömt kühle Luft, es riecht nach Fallobst. In meinem Rücken und zu meiner Linken die geballte Kraft der Bücher, die sich bis unter die hohe Decke stapeln. Auf dem Schreibtisch liegen ein Grundriss der Wohnung und eine Fotografie der Nordwestfassade des Hauses. Sie zeigt einen fein gegliederten, vom Terrain abgesetzten Anbau einer bürgerlichen Villa. Die relativ grossen Fenster des Anbaus, der auch das laubenartige Schlafzimmer beherbergt, sind leicht versetzt zueinander angeordnet, was die Fassade rhythmisiert. Ihr sandgestrahlter Beton verbindet den Anbau auf selbstverständliche Weise mit dem sandfarben verputzten Altbau. Der Umbau der 1929 errichteten Villa zu einem Dreifamilienhaus, dem Haus Wehrli, in dem ich mit meiner Familie seit einer guten Dekade lebe, ist eins der ersten realisierten Projekte von Baumberger & Stegmeier.

Architektur wird, wie Walter Benjamin herausstellt, auf zweifache Weise rezipiert:[1] durch die unterschwellige Wahrnehmung bei ihrem Gebrauch und durch die bewusste Wahrnehmung im Modus der Aufmerksamkeit, wobei Letztere oftmals über Pläne und Fotografien vermittelt ist. Im Gebrauch erfahren wir architektonische Räume als den nicht thematischen Hintergrund der Tätigkeiten, denen wir in ihnen nachgehen. Insbesondere die eigene Wohnung ist durch wiederkehrende Handlungs- und Bewegungsmuster vertraut. Die dabei gemachte Erfahrung ist wesentlich körperlich. Geräusche (wie das das Knarzen der Schwelle) gehen ebenso in sie ein wie taktile Eindrücke (beispielsweise die Kühle der Küche). Die Wahrnehmung erfolgt aber, wie Benjamin festhält, «nicht sowohl auf dem Wege der Aufmerksamkeit als auf dem der Gewohnheit».[2] Und selbst die optische Wahrnehmung findet beim Gebrauch «viel weniger in einem gespannten Aufmerken als in einem beiläufigen Bemerken» statt.[3] Auch visuelle Formen (wie der Kamin mit dem Spiegel) werden nur *en passant* mit peripherem, unscharfem Blick wahrgenommen. Diese erste Rezeptionsform bestimmt unseren alltäglichen Umgang mit Architektur. Die zweite – die bewusste Wahrnehmung im Zustand der Aufmerksamkeit – praktizieren wir nicht nur als Reisende vor berühmten Bauten. Ihr widmen wir uns auch in jenen raren Momenten, in denen wir gewissermassen aus dem Alltag heraustreten und die gebaute Umgebung in den Blick nehmen. Die dabei

PERCEPTION DURING USE AND USING PERCEPTION

Christoph Baumberger

The world behind the glass is silent and bright: the mosaic of houses along the opposite lakeshore appear between the already autumnal trees, while above the woody hilltop, a delicate, unfathomable sky pales towards the horizon, beyond which one's thoughts meander and become indistinct. The espresso-maker hisses and roars as if a distant cavalry were galloping over the ridge. I linger a moment longer by the broad window of the pergola-like bedroom, enjoying the warmth of the afternoon sun, before following the scent of coffee. The kitchen is cool and softly lit. My movements are habitual, my body knows where the hob, cupboard and sink are, allowing my thoughts to wonder while carrying out my simple tasks. I take my coffee with me to the study. The office's narrowness is followed by a sense of lightness and spaciousness; looking down, I avoid the toys on the floor. The living room allows me to walk in a more upright manner. The lake glistens in the mirror above the fireplace, a flash of reflected light shooting through the room like a bright bird. For a moment, I am in an autumnal sea. The threshold to my study makes a familiar creaking sound, as I am enveloped again by subdued light. Cool air flows in through the open window, carrying a scent of fallen fruit; behind me and to the left, a formidable force of books is stacked up towards the high ceiling. A floor plan of the apartment and a photograph of the house's northwestern façade lie on my desk. It presents a finely structured extension to a bourgeois villa that is set apart from the terrain. The large windows of the extension, which also accommodates the pergola-like bedroom, are aligned in a slightly staggered way, thereby giving the façade its rhythm. Its sandblasted concrete naturally connects the extension to the sandy colour of the existing building's plaster. The converted villa known as Wehrli House, which was built in 1929 and now houses three apartments, has been my home for over a decade and is one of the first constructed projects by Baumberger & Stegmeier.

As Walter Benjamin states, architecture is received in two different ways:[1] through subliminal perception while using it and through conscious perception in a mode of awareness, whereby the latter is often communicated using plans and photographs. When using architectural spaces, we experience them as the non-thematic background of activities we carry out within them. Above all, our own home is familiar due to the repeated patterns of behaviour and movement. That experience is primarily physical: sounds (such as the creaking of a threshold) and tactile impressions (e.g. the coolness of the kitchen). However, as Benjamin explains, perception occurs "not so much by way of attention as by way of habit".[2] Even visual perception, when habitual, "spontaneously takes the form of casual noticing, rather than attentive observation."[3] Visual forms (such as the fireplace with a mirror) are only perceived *en passant*, with a peripheral, unfocused view. This initial form of reception determines our daily approach to architecture. We do not only use the second form, namely conscious perception in a condition of awareness, as when we are travellers standing in front of a famous building. We also use it in those rare moments when we step aside from daily life and observe our built surroundings. On

gemachte Erfahrung von Architektur ist fokussiert, distanziert und konzentriert sich oft auf visuelle Eindrücke. In elaborierter Weise kommt sie in der Architekturkritik zur Sprache, die in der Regel der genausten Betrachtung von Details und der Gesamtgestaltung (insbesondere dem Gebäudeäusseren) ein besonderes Gewicht beimisst.[4]

Die beiden Rezeptionsformen legen zwei architektonische Mängel nahe: Ein Gebäude kann schlecht funktionieren, weil es zu viel Aufmerksamkeit in Anspruch nimmt oder weil es die Aufmerksamkeit enttäuscht.[5] Im ersten Fall stört es den alltäglichen Gebrauch, im zweiten Fall beleidigt es die Wahrnehmung. Positiv gewendet ergeben sich zwei Aspekte architektonischer Qualität: Machen wir von einem Gebäude Gebrauch, lässt es uns unsere Aufmerksamkeit; schenken wir ihm Aufmerksamkeit, verhilft es den Ansprüchen der fokussierten Wahrnehmung zu ihrem Recht. Es scheint mir für das Haus Wehrli wie für die späteren, ungleich grösseren Bauten von Baumberger & Stegmeier charakteristisch, dass sie sich durch diese beiden Qualitätsaspekte auszeichnen.

Betrachten wir den ersten Fall etwas genauer. Die Bauten von Baumberger & Stegmeier, bei denen es sich zu einem grossen Teil um Wohnbauten handelt, sind im besten Sinn Alltagsarchitektur. Nun erfahren wir uns im Alltag meist nicht als Subjekte, die ihnen gegenüberstehende Objekte erkennen. Unser primäres Verhältnis zu den Alltagsdingen besteht vielmehr in einem praktisch hantierenden Umgang, bei dem uns die Dinge immer schon als sinnhaft begegnen. Um dies zu verdeutlichen, nennt Martin Heidegger die Gebrauchsdinge «Zeug».[6] Das Wesen des Zeugs besteht darin, dass es zuhanden ist. Es ist da, um etwas mit ihm zu tun und nicht, um angeschaut zu werden. Zwar kann Zeug auch nur angeschaut werden, aber dann ist es nicht im Gebrauch. Das blosse Anschauen (Heidegger nennt es verächtlich «starres Begaffen») macht aus zuhandenen Gebrauchsdingen vorhandene Objekte. Im alltäglichen Umgang geht das Zeug gewissermassen in der Handlung auf, die mit ihm vollzogen wird. Nur wenn der Gebrauch gestört wird, beispielsweise weil das Zeug defekt, funktional unangemessen oder nicht vertraut ist, wird es als solches thematisiert. Zeug ist zudem immer auf anderes Zeug bezogen: Schreibzeug, Papier, Unterlage, Tisch, Lampe, Möbel, Fenster, Türen bilden eine «Zugganzheit». Die Gebrauchsdinge zeigen sich dabei nie zunächst für sich, um dann ein Zimmer auszufüllen. «Das Nächstbegegnende, obzwar nicht thematisch erfasste», so Heidegger, «ist das Zimmer, und dieses wiederum nicht als das ‹Zwischen den vier Wänden› in einem geometrisch räumlichen Sinn – sondern als Wohnzeug. Aus ihm heraus zeigt sich die ‹Einrichtung›, in dieser das jeweils ‹einzelne› Zeug.»[7] Architektur als das einen Raum (das Zimmer) umschliessende Element erweist sich im ungestörten Gebrauch als ebenso unauffällig wie die Dinge in diesem Raum. Ihre Dienlichkeit bestehe deshalb, wie Kirsten Wagner betont, nicht darin, Behälter für diese Dinge zu sein. Architektonische Räume seien vielmehr ordnend, indem sie den Dingen einen ihrer Zuhandenheit gemässen Platz einrichten.[8] Sie setzen die Dinge, ihre Benutzer und die Umgebung in räumliche Beziehungen, die zum Beispiel durch Richtungen, Nähe und Ferne, Öffnungen und Schliessungen sowie Abstufungen zwischen öffentlich und privat bestimmt sind. Zudem schaffen sie durch ihre Konstruktion und Gestaltung Bezüge zur Geschichte und Entwicklung des Gebrauchs und des Orts. Architektur gibt dem Gebrauch also nicht nur einen Raum, sondern strukturiert und orientiert ihn auch, indem sie ihn in räumliche, historische und gesellschaftliche Kontexte einbindet.

Was heisst dies nun für den *ersten* Qualitätsaspekt? Architektur, die zu viel Aufmerksamkeit in Beschlag nimmt, stört den Gebrauch, statt ihn zu orientieren, zum Beispiel, weil sie auf Auffälligkeit setzt oder weil sie ungeeignet ist, die Dinge in eine ihrem

such occasions, our experience of architecture is focused, distanced and often concentrates on visual impressions. This is addressed in an elaborate way in architectural critique, which generally adds particular weight to the precise observation of details and the overall appearance (especially the building exterior).[4]

Both forms of reception indicate two architectural flaws: a building cannot function well because it attracts too much attention, or because it disappoints attention to it.[5] In the first case, it disturbs its everyday utilisation; in the second, it insults perception. Put positively, there are two aspects of architectural quality: when we use a building, it is not obtrusive; when we pay attention to a building, it uses the demands of focused awareness to its advantage. I believe it is a characteristic of Wehrli House and much larger buildings by Baumberger & Stegmeier that they excel in both these quality criteria.

Taking a look at the first more closely: buildings by Baumberger & Stegmeier, which are predominantly housing, are everyday architecture in its best sense. In everyday life, we rarely experience ourselves as subjects that recognise objects before them. Our primary relationship to everyday objects is much more part of practical management, whereby we engage with things that we always already regard as functional. To clarify this, Martin Heidegger describes usable objects as "equipment" (*Zeug*).[6] The nature of such equipment lies in the fact that it is "ready-to-hand". It is there to do something with it, not to look at it. Equipment can also just be looked at, but then it is not in use. Mere observation (Heidegger calls it "rigid gawking") turns things that are "ready-to-hand" into objects that are "present-to-hand". In everyday use, equipment is consumed by activities that are carried out using it. Only if such use is disturbed, for example because the equipment has a defect, is functionally inappropriate or is unfamiliar, does it become thematic as such. Furthermore, equipment always relates to other equipment: stationary, paper, underlays, tables, lamps, furniture, windows and doors form a "totality of equipment". Usable things never show themselves proximally as they are for themselves so as to fill up a room. As Heidegger states, "What we encounter as closest to us (though not as something taken as a theme) is the room; and we encounter it not as something 'between four walls' in a geometrical spatial sense, but as equipment for residing. Out of this the 'arrangement' emerges, and it is in this that any 'individual' item of equipment shows itself."[7] Seen as the elements surrounding a space (the room), architecture is as inconspicuous as the things inside the room when it is used without disturbance. Thus, as Kirsten Wagner stresses, their usefulness does not lie in being vessels for these things. Architectural spaces are much more ordering elements by providing things with a place that is appropriate to their readiness-to-hand.[8] They place things, their users and the surroundings in spatial relationships, which are determined for instance by directions, proximity and distance, openings and closure, as well as gradations between public and private areas. Their construction and design also relate to the history and development of the utilisation, as well as the location. Thus architecture not only provides a space for utilisation, but also structures and orientates it by integrating it into spatial, historical and social contexts.

What does that mean for the *first* quality aspect? Architecture that demands too much attention undermines its utilisation instead of providing orientation,

Gebrauch gemässe Ordnung zu bringen. Dienliche Architektur ist aber nicht gesichtslos. Ihr Charakter, der in der beiläufigen Wahrnehmung unterschwellig erlebt wird, kann durch das Stiften von Bezügen vielmehr zur Orientierung des Gebrauchs beitragen, insbesondere wenn sich einzelne Räume in ihrem Charakter voneinander unterscheiden.[9] Dies ist beim Haus Wehrli der Fall, wo die ursprüngliche Farbigkeit der Wände und des Holzwerks sorgfältig rekonstruiert und modern interpretiert wurde. Die spezifischen Räume mit ihren unterschiedlichen Charakteren verleihen den jeweiligen Tätigkeiten (Kochen, Essen, Spielen, Arbeiten, Schlafen) ein je eigenes Gepräge. Zudem schaffen sie einen Bezug zur Geschichte des Hauses (das traditionelle wie moderne Elemente aufweist), zur Geschichte des Wohnens (die bis ins 20. Jahrhundert eine Geschichte zunehmender Ausdifferenzierung ist) und zur Geschichte der Familie (in deren Besitz sich das Haus seit mehreren Generationen befindet). All diese – und viele weitere – Bezüge strukturieren den Gebrauch, ohne dass sich das Haus deswegen in den Vordergrund drängen würde.

Die vielfältigen Bezüge, die den Gebrauch von Architektur orientieren, bleiben dabei unthematisch. Sie zu thematisieren ist Sache der wachen Aufmerksamkeit. Die beiläufige Wahrnehmung beim Gebrauch weicht dann dem Gebrauch der fokussierten Wahrnehmung. Diese wird nicht enttäuscht, wenn sich die explizit gemachten Bezüge als stimmig erweisen. Dass sich die Bauten von Baumberger & Stegmeier auch durch diesen *zweiten* Qualitätsaspekt auszeichnen, soll anhand weiterer Beispiele angedeutet werden, die zugleich zeigen, wie der Gebrauch eine historische Tiefe erhält. Bei der Wohnüberbauung Brüggliäcker in Zürich-Schwamendingen verbinden zahlreiche formale, inhaltliche und stimmungsmässige Bezüge zur umliegenden Bebauung den genossenschaftlichen Wohnungsbau mit der Idee vom Wohnen in der Gartenstadt. Die geschickt gestaffelten Baukörper gliedern sich ein in die kleinteiligen, unprätentiösen Einfamilien- und Reihenhäuser des von Albert Heinrich Steiner entworfenen Stadtteils. Die simple, teils rot und teils lichtgrau gestrichene Holzschalung, die auf die Moderne der 1950er-Jahre anspielt, unterstützt diesen Bezug ebenso wie der Farbwechsel über die Gebäudekanten, der die Volumina bricht und weniger massiv erscheinen lässt.[10] Auf die Gartenstadtidee verweist auch die feine Abstufung der Nutzungs- und Öffentlichkeitsgrade: Gartenräume, die gemeinschaftlich oder privat genutzt werden können, vermitteln zwischen den öffentlichen Plätzen und den privaten, durch Vorhänge abtrennbaren Aussenräumen der Lauben. Bei der Wohnüberbauung Toblerstrasse in Zürich-Fluntern verbinden die stimmungsmässigen und typologischen Bezüge zum ehemaligen Villenquartier den genossenschaftlichen Siedlungsbau mit dem Ideal des bürgerlichen Wohnens. Die allseitig orientierten, repräsentativen Solitärbauten mit eindeutigen Strassenfassaden verweisen auf die bürgerlichen Wohnhäuser der Umgebung, von denen sie Motive wie die flachen Brüstungsbänder und die blumenfensterartigen Verglasungen aufnehmen und zu einem eigenständigen Ausdruck verdichten. Dieser Bezug wird dadurch unterstützt, dass die sich als Raumkontinuum entwickelnden Wohnungen durch die Vermeidung von Korridoren sowie durch geräumige Eingangsbereiche und vielfältige Zirkulationsmöglichkeiten trotz der knapp bemessenen Fläche eine bürgerliche Grosszügigkeit aufweisen.

Die Bauten von Baumberger & Stegmeier orientieren den Gebrauch nicht nur durch sorgfältig konzipierte Bezüge. Sie schaffen ihm auch Freiräume durch die Realisierung dessen, was Herman Hertzberger «einladende Formen»[11] genannt hat: Angebote für unterschiedliche Nutzungen, die nichts aufzwingen. Die fliessenden Räume an der Toblerstrasse enthalten funktional nicht definierte Bereiche, die sich als Ort für die

for instance by focusing on attracting attention or because it is unsuitable to provide an appropriate order for things in the way they are used. However, useful architecture is not faceless. Its character, which is experienced in its incidental perception, can contribute to orientation by encouraging relationships, especially when individual spaces have contrasting characters.[9] This is the case with Wehrli House, where the original colour of the walls and timber sections have been carefully reconstructed and interpreted in a modern way. The specific spaces with their different characters give the respective activities (such as cooking, eating, working and sleeping) their own qualities. They also relate to the history of the building (which has both traditional and modern elements), the history of living (which until the 20th century was a story of increasing differentiation) and the history of a family (which has owned the building for several generations). All these and many more references structure the building's use, without it becoming obtrusive as a result.

The diverse references that orientate and structure the use of architecture remain non-thematic. Giving them a theme is a matter of focused attention. Thus, incidental perception while using architecture differs from focused perception. The latter is not disappointed if the explicit references prove to be coherent. The fact that buildings by Baumberger & Stegmeier also fulfil this *second* aspect of quality are at least indicated in two other examples. They both show how their utilisation is supplemented by a historical depth. In the case of the Brüggliäcker housing development in Zurich Schwamendingen, numerous formal, content-based and atmospheric references to the surrounding housing connect the cooperative housing estates to the idea of living in a garden city. The skilfully staggered volumes are integrated into the small-scale, unpretentious single-family and terraced housing of the district designed by Albert Heinrich Steiner. The simple, partially red and sometimes light grey-coloured timber cladding, which refers back to 1950s Modernism, supports that reference, as do the alternating colours above the building edges, which break up the volumes and make them appear less massive.[10] The very fine distinctions between levels of use and publicity also point to the idea of a garden city: garden spaces that can be used communally or privately mediate between the public squares and the private exterior areas of the pergolas, which can be partitioned off using curtains. In the case of the housing development in Toblerstrasse, Zurich Fluntern, the atmospheric and typological references to the former villa neighbourhood connect the cooperative housing estates to the ideal of bourgeois residential development. The prestigious free-standing buildings, which are orientated towards all sides and have street façades, refer to the bourgeois housing in the neighbourhood, assuming motifs from it such as the low balustrade bands and the glazing that resembles flower-windows, combining to create an autonomous expression. The reference is strengthened by the fact that the apartments develop as a spatial continuum, whereby the lack of corridors, the roomy entrance areas and diverse circulation possibilities give the apartment a bourgeois spaciousness despite their limited size.

Buildings by Baumberger & Stegmeier do not only orientate their use by carefully conceived references. They also give it leeway by achieving what Hermann Hertzberger calls "inviting forms":[11] potential for different uses

Hausarbeit ebenso anbieten wie als Arbeitsplatz oder Spielbereich und insbesondere dadurch vielfältige Wohnformen erlauben. In den halb öffentlichen Räumen der Siedlung Brüggliäcker markieren in den Boden eingelassene Eichenschwellen, wo Gartenbeete angelegt werden können. Während einige Bewohner das Angebot nutzen, sind andere Schwellen weitgehend überwuchert. Beim Schulhaus Dietlikon verzichteten die Architekten in den Schulzimmern auf die Montage von Bilderschienen und überreichten den Lehrpersonen stattdessen eine Kiste mit Nägeln und Schrauben. Zeichnungen werden direkt an die Wände genagelt, und von den Schrauben ist auch schon Gebrauch gemacht worden, um mit Dachlatten eine Art Hütte in das Schulzimmer einzubauen. Solche Freiheiten ermöglichen die Aneignung von Architektur. Sich einen Ort zu eigen zu machen, bedeutet nicht nur, die durch seine räumliche Ordnung und architektonische Gestaltung evozierten Umgangsweisen zu verinnerlichen; es ist immer auch mit Formen des Eingreifens, Markierens und Umgestaltens verbunden.[12] Über solche Aneignungsspielräume wiederum trägt die Architektur von Baumberger & Stegmeier zur Entfaltung der Identität ihrer Benutzer bei, da sich Identitäten in der aktiven Auseinandersetzung mit der Umwelt entwickeln, zu der auch die gebaute Umwelt gehört.

Nach getaner Arbeit verlasse ich mein dämmriges Labor für die allmähliche Verfertigung der Gedanken beim Schreiben und trete hinaus auf die sienarote Loggia, die offen ist gegen den Garten, wo die Kinder Fussball spielen. Samstagabend, Herbstluft, Erdgeruch. Auf dem mächtigen Holztisch einige Äpfel und Feigen. Aus dem Gemüsegarten gelegentlich der helle Klang, wenn die Spitzhacke auf Stein trifft. Zwischen den Glyzinien der See im letzten Licht des Tags. Herbstmeer. An der sandfarbenen Altbaufassade wächst der Wein hoch. Gegenüber der Loggia steht als ihr Pendant der Anbau mit der Terrasse, von der her man leise die Stimmen der Nachbarn hört, die Besuch haben. Alles da. Das Haus, denke ich dankbar, verankert mich in der Zeit und richtet mich aus. Es steht hinter mir, verbindet mich mit dem, was war, und öffnet mich für das, was kommt.

1. Walter Benjamin: Das Kunstwerk im Zeitalter seiner technischen Reproduzierbarkeit. In: ders.: Gesammelte Schriften, Bd. 1.2. Frankfurt am Main: Suhrkamp 1991. S. 431–469, hier S. 465.
2. Ebd.
3. Ebd.
4. Martin Doll: Architekturwahrnehmung im Gebrauch. In: Sabine Ammon u.a. (Hg.), Architektur im Gebrauch. Gebaute Umwelt als Lebenswelt. Berlin: Universitätsverlag der TU Berlin 2018. S. 122–137.
5. Georg Franck und Dorothea Franck: Architektonische Qualität. München: Hanser 2008. S. 23.
6. Martin Heidegger: Sein und Zeit. Tübingen: Niemeyer 1993. §§ 15–16, S. 66–76.
7. Ebd., S. 68.
8. Kirsten Wagner: Hermeneutiken des Architekturgebrauchs. In: Sebastian Feldhusen und Ute Poerschke (Hg.), Theorie der Architektur. Zeitgenössische Positionen. Basel: Birkhäuser 2017. S. 410–435, insbesondere S. 420.
9. Ich spreche von «Charakter» statt von «Atmosphäre», da diese viel flüchtiger und stärker an die Oberfläche gebunden ist; vgl. Christoph Baumberger und Georg Brun: Identität, Charakter und Stil von Bauwerken. In: Christoph Baumberger (Hg.), Architekturphilosophie. Grundlagentexte. Münster: Mentis 2013. S. 141–166.
10. Die Bezüge werden aber nie ideologisch durchgehalten, sondern sind oft von heiterer Mehrdeutigkeit: So spielt das Rot der Holzschalung nicht nur auf die Steiner-Moderne der 1950er-Jahre an, sondern evoziert auch schwedische Landhäuser. Und das Grün im Bereich der Treppenhäuser verweist nicht nur auf die brachialere Moderne von Le Corbusiers Unité d'habitation, es ist zugleich eine verfremdete Anspielung auf das Fensterladengrün der umliegenden Einfamilien- und Reihenhäuser.
11. Herman Hertzberger: Vom Bauen. Vorlesungen über Architektur. München: Aries 1995. S. 173.
12. Silke Steets: Der sinnhafte Aufbau der gebauten Welt. Eine Architektursoziologie. Frankfurt am Main: Suhrkamp 2015. Kapitel 5.

without imposing anything upon people. The fluent spaces along Toblerstrasse contain functionally undefined areas, providing space for household tasks, a workplace or a playing area, thereby enabling a diversity of residential forms. In the semi-open spaces of the Brüggliäcker estate, oak thresholds sunken into the ground mark where garden beds can be developed. While some residents take the opportunity, other thresholds are largely overgrown. In the case of the Dietlikon school building, the architects decided against fitting picture rails in the classrooms, instead handing the teachers a box with nails and screws. Drawings are nailed directly onto the walls. Screws were also used, as roof battens were connected to build a kind of cabin in the classroom. Such liberties enable the appropriation of architecture. Making a place one's own not only means internalising the behaviour evoked by its spatial order and architectural design; it always also involves forms of intervention, marking and conversion.[12] Architecture by Baumberger & Stegmeier adds to the users' identity-building potential through such leeway of appropriation, since identities develop in the active engagement with their environment, including the built surroundings.

After completing my work, I leave my dusky laboratory to the gradual consolidation of my thoughts in writing, step out into the loggia, which opens out towards the garden, where the children are playing football. Saturday evening, autumn air, the scent of earth. Some apples and a few figs are on the mighty dining table. Occasionally, the light sound of a pickaxe can be heard as it strikes a stone. The lake is visible behind the wisteria in the twilight. An autumnal sea. Vines creep high upon the building's sandy-coloured old façade. The loggia faces its counterpart, the extension with a terrace, from where the neighbours' soft voices emanate. They are entertaining guests. Everything is here. I gratefully understand that the house anchors me in time and provides orientation. It is behind me, connecting me with what was and opening me to what lies ahead.

1. Walter Benjamin: "The Work of Art in the Age of its Technological Reproduction". In: Selected Writings, Volume 3, 1935–1938, translated by Edmund Jephcott, Howard Eiland et al.; Howard Eiland and Michael W. Jennings (Eds.). Cambridge, Mass; London, England: The Belknap Press of Harvard University Press 2002, p. 101–142, here p. 120.
2. Ibid. p. 120
3. Ibid. p. 120
4. Martin Doll: "Architekturwahrnehmung im Gebrauch". In: Sabine Ammon et al. (Eds.), Architektur im Gebrauch. Gebaute Umwelt als Lebenswelt. Berlin: Universitätsverlag der TU Berlin 2018, p. 122–137.
5. Georg Franck and Dorothea Franck: Architektonische Qualität. Munich: Hanser 2008, p. 23.
6. Martin Heidegger: Time and Being, translated by John Macquarrie & Edward Robinson. Oxford UK, Cambridge, USA 1962.
7. Ibid. p. 98.
8. Kirsten Wagner: "Hermeneutiken des Architekturgebrauchs". In: Sebastian Feldhusen and Ute Poerschke (Eds.), Theorie der Architektur. Zeitgenössische Positionen. Basel: Birkhäuser 2017, p. 410–435, esp. p. 420.
9. The word "character" is used here deliberately rather than "atmosphere", since the latter is much more fleeting and more strongly connected to the surface; cf. Christoph Baumberger and Georg Brun: "Identität, Charakter und Stil von Bauwerken". In: Christoph Baumberger (Ed.), Architekturphilosophie. Grundlagentexte. Münster: Mentis 2013, p. 141–166.
10. However, the references are never adhered to ideologically and often include playful ambiguity: for instance, the red colour of the cladding not only refers to Steiner's 1950s Modernism, but also evokes Swedish country cottages. Likewise, the green in the area of the staircases refers not only to the more forceful Modernism of Le Corbusier's Unité d'habitation, but is also an alienated reflection of the green shutters used by the surrounding single-family homes and terraced houses.
11. Hermann Hertzberger: Vom Bauen. Vorlesungen über Architektur. Munich: Aries 1995, p. 173.
12. Silke Steets: Der sinnhafte Aufbau der gebauten Welt. Eine Architektursoziologie. Frankfurt a. M.: Suhrkamp 2015, Ch. 5.

WERKVERZEICHNIS
Auswahl Bauten, Projekte und Wettbewerbe

2003   1   Wettbewerb Sonderschulheim, Scharans; 1. Ankauf
Wettbewerb Primarschule Rebhügel, Zürich; 2. Preis

2004   Wettbewerb Schulanlage, Boppelsen; 4. Preis
Wettbewerb Erweiterung Kantonsschule, Baldegg; 3. Preis
   2   Wettbewerb Neubau Primarschulhaus, Oetwil am See; 4. Preis

2005   Primarschulhaus Blattenacher, Oetwil am See (Wettbewerb 2004, 1. Preis)
An- und Umbau Einfamilienhaus, Pfäffikon (Direktauftrag)
Wettbewerb Wohnüberbauung Zelgli, Winterthur (mit KilgaPopp Architekten)
Projektstudie Einfamilienhaus, Magden

2007   An- und Umbau Haus Wehrli, Zollikon (Direktauftrag)
   3   Wettbewerb Neubau Appartementresidenz, Uetikon am See; 2. Preis
Städtebauliches Leitbild Klinik Schlössli, Oetwil am See

2009   Wettbewerb Alterszentrum, Maienfeld
   4   Wettbewerb Alterszentrum, Vella; 6. Preis
Wettbewerb Bildungszentrum Rüterwies, Zollikerberg; 4. Preis*

2010   Mehrfamilienhaus Segantinistrasse, Zürich-Höngg (Direktauftrag)
   5   Mehrfamilienhaus Bahnhofstrasse, Zollikon (Direktauftrag)

2011   6   Wettbewerb Schulanlage Blumenfeld, Zürich-Affoltern; 2. Preis*

2012   Wettbewerb Wohnüberbauung Friesenberg, Zürich*
   7   Studienauftrag Stadthaus Metzgerhalle, Zürich-Oerlikon*
Wettbewerb Wohnüberbauung mit Gewerbeanteil Manegg-Greencity, Zürich*

2013   Primarschulzentrum, Laufen (Wettbewerb 2007, 1. Preis)
Wohnüberbauung Katzenbach, Etappe III, Zürich-Seebach (Wettbewerb 2010, 1. Preis)*
Studienauftrag Areal Bülachguss, Bülach*
Studienauftrag Gesamtüberbauung Schafschürwies, Feldbach; 1. Preis*
Studienauftrag Labitzke Areal, Zürich*

2014   Schulanlage Dorf, Dietlikon (Wettbewerb 2008, 1. Preis)
Wohnüberbauung Brüggliäcker, Zürich-Schwamendingen (Wettbewerb 2009, 1. Preis)*
   8   Wettbewerb Schulhaus Dietlimoos, Adliswil; 3. Preis
   9   Wettbewerb Alterswohnsiedlung Rebbüehl, Uster; 4. Preis
  10   Wettbewerb Wohnsiedlung Vogelsang, Winterthur; 2. Preis*
  11   Wettbewerb Wohnüberbauung Bellariarain, Zürich*

2015   Private Altersklinik Bergheim, Uetikon am See (Direktauftrag 2009)
Wettbewerb Wohnüberbauung Am Rain, Brugg; 3. Preis
  12   Wettbewerb Mehrzwecksaal Obere Mühle, Dübendorf; 2. Preis
  13   Wettbewerb Wohn- und Gewerbeüberbauung Zollhaus, Zürich; 9. Preis*
Wohnüberbauung Guggach, Zürich-Oerlikon (Wettbewerb 2011, 1. Preis)*
  14   Wettbewerb Wohnsiedlung Letzibach D, Zürich; 5. Preis*
Wohnüberbauung Katzenbach, Etappe IV, Zürich-Seebach (Wettbewerb 2010, 1. Preis)*

2016   Multifunktionales Wohnhaus, Oetwil am See (Wettbewerb 2013, 1. Preis)
Wettbewerb Citycenter Rapperswil*
Workshopverfahren Verdichtungsstrategien Nordtangente*
  15   Wettbewerb Entenbad, Dietikon*
Wettbewerb Wohnhaus Letzi, Zürich; 3. Preis*
  16   Wettbewerb Schulraumerweiterung und Neubau Mehrzweckhalle, Kirchberg; 3. Preis
Arealüberbauung Guggach, Zürich-Unterstrass (Wettbewerb 2011, 1. Preis)*
Wohnhaus Marti, Schwanden (Direktauftrag 2014)

2017   Wohnsiedlung Toblerstrasse, Zürich-Fluntern (Wettbewerb 2010, 1. Preis)*
Wettbewerb Wohnüberbauung Herzogenmühle, Zürich*
Wettbewerb Birchstrasse, Zürich-Oerlikon*
Studienauftrag Pilatus Arena Kriens*
Studienauftrag Bahnhofsareal Ost, Rotkreuz*

1

2

3

4

5

6

7

8

9

10

LIST OF WORKS
Selected buildings, projects and competitions

2003	1	Competition, special residential school, Scharans; 1st Purchase
		Competition, Rebhügel primary school, Zurich; 2nd Prize
2004		Competition, school facility, Boppelsen; 4th Prize
		Competition, cantonal school extension, Baldegg; 3rd Prize
	2	Competition, new primary school building, Oetwil am See; 4th Prize
2005		Blattenacher primary school, Oetwil am See (competition in 2004, 1st Prize)
		Extension and conversion of a single-family home, Pfäffikon (direct contract)
		Competition, Zelgli housing development, Winterthur (with KilgaPopp Architekten)
		Project study, single-family home, Magden
2007		Extension and conversion of Wehrli House, Zollikon (direct contract)
	3	Competition, new apartment building, Uetikon am See; 2nd Prize
		Urban-planning model, Klinik Schlössli, Oetwil am See
2009		Competition, centre for the elderly, Maienfeld
	4	Competition, centre for the elderly, Vella; 6th Prize
		Competition, Rüterwies education centre, Zollikerberg; 4th Prize*
2010		Segantinistrasse apartment building, Zurich-Höngg (direct contract)
	5	Bahnhofstrasse apartment building, Zollikon (direct contract)
2011	6	Competition, Blumenfeld school facility, Zurich Affoltern; 2nd Prize*
2012		Competition, Friesenberg housing development, Zurich*
	7	Study contract, Metzgerhalle townhouse, Zurich-Oerlikon*
		Competition, housing development with commercial units, Manegg-Greencity, Zurich*
2013		Primary school centre, Laufen (competition in 2007, 1st Prize)
		Katzenbach housing development, Stage III, Zurich-Seebach (competition in 2010, 1st Prize)*
		Study contract, Areal Bülachguss, Bülach*
		Study contract, general development, Schafschürwies, Feldbach; 1st Prize*
		Study contract, Labitzke Areal, Zurich*
2014		Dorf school facility, Dietlikon (competition in 2008, 1st Prize)
		Brüggliäcker housing development, Zurich-Schwamendingen (competition in 2009, 1st Prize)*
	8	Competition, Dietlimoos school building, Adliswil; 3rd Prize
	9	Competition, Rehbüehl centre for the elderly, Uster; 4th Prize
	10	Competition, Vogelsang housing estate, Winterthur; 2nd Prize*
	11	Competition, Bellariarain housing development, Zurich*
2015		Bergheim private geriatric clinic, Uetikon am See (direct contract in 2009)
		Competition, Am Rain housing development, Brugg; 3rd Prize
	12	Competition, Obere Mühle multifunctional hall, Dübendorf; 2nd Prize
	13	Competition, Zollhaus housing and commercial development, Zurich; 9th Prize*
		Guggach housing development, Zurich-Oerlikon (competition in 2011, 1st Prize)*
	14	Competition, Letzibach D housing estate, Zurich; 5th Prize*
		Katzenbach housing development, Stage IV, Zurich-Seebach (competition in 2010, 1st Prize)*
2016		Multifunctional residential building, Oetwil am See (competition in 2013, 1st Prize)
		Competition, Citycenter Rapperswil*
		Workshop process, densification strategies, Nordtangente*
	15	Competition, Entenbad, Dietikon*
		Competition, Letzi residential building, Zurich; 3rd Prize*
	16	Competition, school extension and new multifunctional hall, Kirchberg; 3rd Prize
		Guggach site development, Zurich-Unterstrass (competition in 2011, 1st Prize)*
		Marti residential building, Schwanden (direct contract in 2014)

2018	Projektwettbewerb Schwimmhalle Neufeld, Bern; 3. Rang/1. Ankauf Wettbewerb Neu- und Umbauten Bucherareal, Burgdorf* Studienauftrag Baufeld Nord, Ziegeleipark-Areal, Horw Mehrfamilienhaus Ottikerstrasse, Zürich (Direktauftrag 2014) Studienauftrag Universitätsspital Zürich*	
2019	Wettbewerb Bildungszentrum Grevas, St. Moritz; 5. Preis* Wettbewerb Kochareal, Zürich* Wettbewerb Wohn- und Alterszentrum Adliswil* Appartementhäuser, Andermatt (Wettbewerb 2016. 1. Preis; mit Miller & Maranta) Wohnüberbauung am Katzenbach, Etappe V, Zürich-Seebach (Wettbewerb 2010, 1. Preis)* Wohnüberbauung Am Chatzebach, Muri (Studienauftrag 2016, 1. Preis) Wettbewerb Schulanlage Kleinholz, Olten* Wettbewerb Heinrichareal, Zürich*	 11
	Laufende Projekte	
17	Zentrumsentwicklung Geroldswil (Wettbewerb 2014, 1. Preis) Wohnsiedlung Schwamendinger-Dreieck, Zürich-Schwamendingen (Wettbewerb 2014, 1. Preis)*	
18	Neubau Witikonerstrasse, Zürich (Studienauftrag 2015, 1. Preis) Lokstadt, Winterthur (Wettbewerb 2016, 1. Preis) Wohnüberbauung Storchensiedlung, Oetwil am See (Wettbewerb 2018, 1. Preis) Gemeindezentrum Geroldswil (Studienauftrag 2018, 1. Preis)	
19	Ersatzneubauten Riedacker, Zürich (Wettbewerb 2018, 1. Preis)* Sekundarschulhaus Chliriet, Rümlang-Oberglatt (Wettbewerb 2018, 1. Preis)* Feldmühleareal, Rorschach (Studienauftrag 2018, 1. Preis) Wohnhaus Ehrendingerstrasse, Ennetbaden (Direktauftrag 2018) Wohnüberbauung Hofwisen, Niederhasli (Studienauftrag 2018, 1. Preis)	12
20	Wohnheim Areal Gotthardstall, Einsiedeln (Wettbewerb 2019, 1. Preis) Wohnsiedlung Buchwiesen, Zürich (Wettbewerb 2019, 1. Preis)*	

* BS+EMI Architektenpartner (in Zusammenarbeit mit Edelaar Mosayebi Inderbitzin Architekten, Zürich)

13

14

15

16

17

18

20

2017	Toblerstrasse housing estate, Zurich-Fluntern (competition in 2010, 1st Prize)*
	Competition, Herzogenmühle housing development, Zurich*
	Competition, Birchstrasse, Zurich-Oerlikon*
	Study contract, Pilatus Arena Kriens*
	Study contract, Bahnhofsareal Ost, Rotkreuz*
2018	Projekt competition, Neufeld indoor swimming facility, Bern; 3rd Prize /1st Purchase
	Competition, new development and conversion, Bucherareal, Burgdorf*
	Study contract, Baufeld Nord, Ziegeleipark-Areal, Horw
	Ottikerstrasse apartment building, Zurich (direct contract in 2014)
	Study contract, Zurich University Hospital*
2019	Competition, Grevas educational centre, St. Moritz; 5th Prize*
	Competition, Kochareal, Zurich*
	Competition, residential and senior citizens' centre, Adliswil*
	Apartment buildings, Andermatt (competition in 2016. 1st Prize; with Miller & Maranta)
	Katzenbach housing development, Stage V, Zurich-Seebach (competition in 2010, 1st Prize)*
	Am Chatzebach housing development, Muri (study contract in 2016, 1st Prize)
	Competition, Kleinholz school facility, Olten*
	Competition, Heinrichareal, Zurich*

Current projects

17 Geroldswil centre development (competition in 2014, 1st Prize)
    Schwamendinger-Dreieck housing estate, Zurich (competition in 2014, 1st Prize)*
18 New building in Witikonerstrasse, Zurich (study contract in 2015, 1st Prize)
    Lokstadt, Winterthur (competition in 2016, 1st Prize)
    Storchensiedlung housing development, Oetwil am See (competition in 2018, 1st Prize)
    Geroldswil municipal centre (study contract in 2018, 1st Prize)
19 Riedacker replacement building, Zurich (competition in 2018, 1st Prize)*
    Chliriet secondary school, Rümlang-Oberglatt (competition in 2018, 1st Prize)*
    Feldmühleareal, Rorschach (study contract in 2018, 1st Prize)
    Ehrendingerstrasse residential building, Ennetbaden (direct contract, 2018)
    Hofwisen housing development, Niederhasli (study contract in 2018, 1st Prize)
20 Areal Gotthardstall residential care centre, Einsiedeln (competition in 2019, 1st Prize)
    Buchwiesen housing estate, Zurich (competition in 2019, 1st Prize)*

* BS+EMI Architektenpartner (in collaboration with Edelaar Mosayebi Inderbitzin Architekten, Zurich)

KARIN STEGMEIER

1966	geboren in Zürich
1988–1994	Architekturstudium an der ETH Zürich, Diplom bei Prof. Hans Kollhoff
1994–1995	Mitarbeit bei Gioni Signorell, Chur
1996–1997	Nachdiplomstudium Architekturtheorie bei Prof. Kurt W. Forster, ETH Zürich
1997–1998	Mitarbeit bei Stücheli Architekten, Zürich
1999	Mitarbeit bei Dürig & Rämi Architekten, Zürich
2000–2005	Assistenz am Lehrstuhl Prof. Adrian Meyer, ETH Zürich
2001–2002	eigenes Büro
2003–	gemeinsames Büro mit Peter Baumberger in Zürich
2003–	Firmenmitglied im SIA (Schweizerischer Ingenieur- und Architektenverein)
2011	Gründung BS+EMI Architektenpartner AG
2013–	Mitglied im BSA (Bund Schweizer Architekten)

PETER BAUMBERGER

1969	geboren in Zürich
1986–1990	Ausbildung als Hochbauzeichner
1991	Mitarbeit im Architekturbüro Prof. Roland Leu, Wetzikon
1991–1995	Architekturstudium am Technikum Winterthur
1994	Mitarbeit bei Gigon Guyer Architekten, Zürich
1995–1996	Mitarbeit bei Graber Pulver Architekten, Zürich
1996–2005	Mitarbeit bei Miller & Maranta, Basel
2001–2003	Assistenz bei Gastprofessor Florian Riegler, ETH Zürich
2003–	gemeinsames Büro mit Karin Stegmeier in Zürich
2003–	Firmenmitglied im SIA (Schweizerischer Ingenieur- und Architektenverein)
2011	Gründung BS+EMI Architektenpartner AG
2012–	Vorstandsmitglied des SIA FEB (Fachgruppe für die Erhaltung von Bauwerken)
2013–	Mitglied im BSA (Bund Schweizer Architekten)

ERWEITERTE GESCHÄFTSLEITUNG

Daniel Kaschub, Mirko Schlemminger

MITARBEITENDE

aktuell Falk Ahlhelm, Gamze Atas, Deborah Augsburger, Boris Borrelli, Arno Bruderer, Timo Bullmann, Yannick Charpié, Julian Daniel*, Kevin Dröscher*, Sarah Fahrni, Michael Fehlmann, Nils Franzini*, Roger Frick, Peter Gaub*, Andrea Grolimund*, Manuel Hödl*, Aurelia Huber, Patric Hütter*, Nadine Jaberg, Michael Kälin, Sovachana Keo, Stephanie Knerr, Caroline Lütjens, Thomas Luchsinger, Stephan Mauser*, Jules Mignot, Viola Müller, Lou Münger*, Charel Muller*, Alexandra Niedermayr, Anna Oexle*, Katrin Pfäffli*, Remo Reichmuth, Marius Rinderknecht, Michelle Rojas, Charlotte Samtleben*, Anouk Schepens, Manuela Schneeberger, Roman Schober, Marta Shtipkova-Michael, Daniel Sigrist, Katharina Sommer*, Corinne Späni, Michael Stirnemann*, Phillip Türich*, Julia Werlberger*, Mike Zweidler

ehemalig Dominic Aeberhard*, Denis Benetas, Rosalyn Bermudez, Anika Börger, Florian Boettcher*, Michael Brotzer*, Manuel Burkhardt*, Margret Bust, Jenna Buttermann*, Giancarlo Ceriani, Ronan Crippa*, Donatella Cugini, Zsuzsanna Edes, Julian Fischer*, Désirée Flury, Sandra Frei*, Claudia Freiburghaus, Corinne Fuchs, Reto Gasser*, Manfred Gulcz, Thorsten Haack*, Laurenz Härtl, Nora Iannone*, Marisa Imgrüt, Mathis Keller*, Katharina Kiesbauer*, Clemens Klötzer, Carolin Kubat*, Laura Kübler, Julia Lang*, Andrea Linke*, Michael Mader*, Severin Marti, Amos Mauri*, Katja Mayer, Lorenz Mörikofer, Jens Nehring*, Livia Notarangelo, Irina Österrreicher, Luca Pestalozzi*, Stephan Pfeiffer*, Petros Polychronis, Patricia Quinte, Mihai Radulescu*, Hella Raue, Celestin Rohner*, Alexandra Scheibl, Peter Schend*, Juliana Schenk*, Lars Schriever, Thomas Schiratzki*, Dennis Schlatter, Nathalie Schümperlin, Anna Schork*, Michele Schweri, Franziska Singer*, Laurina Sponagel, Simon Staudacher, Pascal Steiner*, Gian-Carlo Tibolla, Thomas Toffel*, Lukas Vogt*, Esther Vonwil, Deborah Wyss*, Kristina Zentgraf, Lichen Zhu, Andreas Zimmerli*

* bei BS+EMI Architektenpartner

AUSZEICHNUNGEN

2013	Arc-Award 13 (Sonderpreis Ingenieurleistung), Schulanlage Dorf Dietlikon
2015	best architects 15 (Auszeichnung Gold), Primarschulzentrum Laufen
	best architects 15, Schulanlage Dorf Dietlikon
	best architects 15, Mehrfamilienhaus Segantini
2016	best architects 17, Wohnüberbauung Guggach
	best architects 17, Wohnüberbauung am Katzenbach III
	Arc-Award 16 Gold (Kategorie Wohnbauten), Wohnsiedlung Brüggliäcker
2018	Gute Bauten Kanton Basel-Landschaft/Kanton Basel-Stadt Primarschulzentrum Laufen
	best architects 19, Wohnsiedlung Toblerstrasse

BIBLIOGRAFIE (AUSWAHL)

2007	Viel Glas zwischen Reben und Stadt. In: baz, 19.12.2007/land
	Alexander Felix: Wettbewerb Primarschulzentrum Laufen. In: TEC21, 44/2007, S. 8–9
2008	Das Schulhaus wird auf Fels gebaut. In: baz, 27.02.2008/land
2009	Neue Wohnsiedlung in Schwamendingen. In: Neue Zürcher Zeitung, 01.07.2009, S. 47
	70 Wohnungen für die Gartenstadt Schwamendingen (Wohnsiedlung Brüggliäcker). In: Tages-Anzeiger, 30.06.2009
	Wettbewerb Schulhauserweiterung Dietlikon. In: TEC21, 16/2009, S. 8
2010	Neue Wohnungen am Katzenbach. In: Tages-Anzeiger, 15.03.2010, S. 19

KARIN STEGMEIER

1966	Born in Zurich
1988–1994	Studied Architecture at the ETH Zurich, graduating under Prof. Hans Kollhoff
1994–1995	Employed by G. Signorell, Chur
1996–1997	Post-graduate studies in Architectural Theory under Prof. Kurt W. Forster, ETH Zurich
1997–1998	Employed by Stücheli Architekten, Zurich
1999	Employed by Dürig & Rämi Architekten, Zurich
2000–2005	Assistant at the Chair of Prof. Adrian Meyer, ETH Zurich
2001–2002	Own office
2003–	Joint office with Peter Baumberger in Zurich
2003–	SIA (Swiss Society of Engineers and Architects) corporate member
2011	Founded BS+EMI Architektenpartner AG
2013–	Member, Federation of Swiss Architects (BSA)

PETER BAUMBERGER

1969	Born in Zurich
1986–1990	Apprenticeship as a draughtsman
1991	Employed by the architectural office of Prof. R. Leu, Wetzikon
1991–1995	Studied Architecture at the Technikum Winterthur
1994	Employed by Gigon / Guyer Architekten, Zurich
1995–1996	Employed by Graber Pulver Architekten, Zurich
1996–2005	Employed by Miller & Maranta, Basel
2001–2003	Assistant to Guest Professor Florian Riegler, ETH Zurich
2003–	Joint office with Karin Stegmeier in Zurich
2003–	SIA (Swiss Society of Engineers and Architects) corporate member
2011	Founded BS+EMI Architektenpartner AG
2012–	SIA FEB (specialist group for building preservation) Board Member
2013–	Member, Federation of Swiss Architects (BSA)

EXTENDED MANAGEMENT

Daniel Kaschub, Mirko Schlemminger

TEAM

current: Falk Ahlhelm, Gamze Atas, Deborah Augsburger, Boris Borrelli, Arno Bruderer, Timo Bullmann, Yannick Charpié, Julian Daniel*, Kevin Dröscher*, Sarah Fahrni, Michael Fehlmann, Nils Franzini*, Roger Frick, Peter Gaub*, Andrea Grolimund*, Manuel Hödl*, Aurelia Huber, Patric Hütter*, Nadine Jaberg, Michael Kälin, Sovachana Keo, Stephanie Knerr, Thomas Luchsinger, Caroline Lütjens, Stephan Mauser*, Jules Mignot, Charel Muller*, Viola Müller, Lou Münger*, Alexandra Niedermayr, Anna Oexle*, Katrin Pfäffli*, Remo Reichmuth, Marius Rinderknecht, Michelle Rojas, Charlotte Samtleben*, Anouk Schepens, Manuela Schneeberger, Roman Schober, Marta Shtipkova-Michael, Daniel Sigrist, Katharina Sommer*, Corinne Späni, Michael Stirnemann*, Phillip Türich*, Julia Werlberger*, Mike Zweidler

former: Dominic Aeberhard*, Denis Benetas, Rosalyn Bermudez, Florian Boettcher*, Anika Börger, Michael Brotzer*, Manuel Burkhardt*, Margret Bust, Jenna Buttermann*, Giancarlo Ceriani, Ronan Crippa*, Donatella Cugini, Zsuzsanna Edes, Julian Fischer*, Désirée Flury, Sandra Frei*, Claudia Freiburghaus, Corinne Fuchs, Reto Gasser*, Manfred Gulcz, Thorsten Haack*, Laurenz Härtl, Nora Iannone*, Marisa Imgrüt, Mathis Keller*, Katharina Kiesbauer*, Clemens Klötzer, Carolin Kubat*, Laura Kübler, Julia Lang*, Andrea Linke*, Michael Mader*, Severin Marti, Amos Mauri*, Katja Mayer, Lorenz Mörikofer, Jens Nehring*, Livia Notarangelo, Irina Österrreicher, Luca Pestalozzi*, Stephan Pfeiffer*, Petros Polychronis, Patricia Quinte, Mihai Radulescu*, Hella Raue, Celestin Rohner*, Alexandra Scheibl, Peter Schend*, Juliana Schenk*, Lars Schriever, Thomas Schiratzki*, Dennis Schlatter, Nathalie Schümperlin, Anna Schork*, Michele Schweri, Franziska Singer*, Laurina Sponagel, Simon Staudacher, Pascal Steiner*, Gian-Carlo Tibolla, Thomas Toffel*, Lukas Vogt*, Esther Vonwil, Deborah Wyss*, Kristina Zentgraf, Lichen Zhu, Andreas Zimmerli*

* in BS+EMI Architektenpartner

AWARDS

2013	Arc-Award 13 (Special Prize for Engineering) Dietlikon school building
2015	best architects 15 (Gold Award), Laufen primary school
	best architects 15, Dietlikon school building
	best architects 15, Segantini apartment building
2016	best architects 17, Guggach housing development
	best architects 17, Am Katzenbach III housing estate
	Arc-Award 16 Gold (residential category), Brüggliäcker housing development
2018	Gute Bauten Kanton Basel-Landschaft/Kanton Basel-Stadt, Laufen primary school
	best architects 19, Toblerstrasse housing estate

BIBLIOGRAPHY (SELECTED)

2007	"Viel Glas zwischen Reben und Stadt". In: *baz* 19.12.2007/land
	Alexander Felix: "Wettbewerb, Primarschulzentrum Laufen". In: *TEC21* 44/2007, p. 8–9
2008	"Das Schulhaus wird auf Fels gebaut". In: *baz* 27.2.2008/land
2009	"Neue Wohnsiedlung in Schwamendingen". In: *Neue Zürcher Zeitung*, 1.7.2009, p. 47
	"70 Wohnungen für die Gartenstadt Schwamendingen" (Brüggliäcker housing estate). In: *Tages-Anzeiger*, 30.6.2009
	"Wettbewerb, Schulhauserweiterung Dietlikon". In: *TEC21* 16/2009, p. 8

2011	Martin Tschanz: Kultivierte Wohnlichkeit (Mehrfamilienhaus Segantini). In: werk, bauen + wohnen 12/2011, S. 58–59.
	Ivo Bösch: Die stillen Gewinner. Ein Architektenteam gewinnt sechs Wohnbauwettbewerbe. In: Hochparterre 5/2011, S. 44–45
	Paul Knüsel: Gartenstadt reloaded (Wohnüberbauung am Katzenbach III–V). In: faktor 29/2011, S. 8–10
2012	David Ganzoni: Wie liest man einen Grundrissplan? Die Gute Wohnung (Wohnsiedlung Brüggliäcker). In: Wohnen 5/2012, S. 26–29
	Leben mit Ecken und Kanten (Mehrfamilienhaus Segantini). In: Sonntags Zeitung, 29.03.2012, S. 63
2013	Peter Popp: Subtile Raumbildung: Schulhaus und Gemeindebibliothek in Dietlikon: www.detail.de, 17.12.2013
2014	Richard Liechti: Mit Bedacht verdichtet (Wohnsiedlung Brüggliäcker). In: Wohnen 11/2014, S. 22–25
	Andreas Kohne: Die Gartenstadt für morgen (Wohnsiedlung Schwamendinger-Dreieck). In: TEC21 45/2014, S. 8–10
	Primarschulzentrum Laufen. In: AS Schweizer Architektur 195, 4/2014, S. 7–10
	Grundrissfibel Alterszentren 44 Architekturwettbewerbe in der Schweiz 2002–2014, Zürich 2014
	Andres Herzog: Zickzack unter dem Kostendach (Primarschulzentrum Laufen). In: Hochparterre 3/2014, S. 22–27
	Roland Züger: Vom Dorf ein Bild machen (Schulanlage Dorf Dietlikon). In: werk, bauen + wohnen 1/2, 2014, S. 76
2015	Marcel Bächtiger: Rhetorik und Realität (Wettbewerb Zentrumsentwicklung Geroldswil): www.hochparterre.ch, 19.08.2015
	Grundrissfibel Schulbauten 30 Wettbewerbe in der Schweiz 2001–2015 (Primarschulzentrum Laufen, Schulanlage Blumenfeld), Zürich 2015
2016	Marianne Kürsteiner: Conserver son caractère à l'image de la ville-jardin (Wohnsiedlung Brüggliäcker). In: idea 6/2016, S. 46–49
	Christophe Joud: Porte, Une scénographie des passages (Wohnsiedlung Brüggliäcker). In: cahier de théorie, A l'intérieur 13/2016, S. 79–91
	Christian Inderbitzin und Elli Mosayebi: La porte, une échelle de l'habitat. In: matières 13/2016, S. 86–97
	Schulanlage Dorf Dietlikon. In: Lignum Construction bois – Ecoles 14/2016, S. 46/47
	Agnès Laube und Michael Widrig: Archigrafie. Schrift am Bau (Schulanlage Dorf Dietlikon), Basel u. a. 2016
	Emma Letizia Jones und Philip Shelley: How housing co-operatives built a city (Wohnsiedlung Brüggliäcker, Wettbewerb Wohn- und Gewerbeüberbauung Zollstrasse): www.architectural-review.com, 04.10.2016
2017	Werner Huber: Krokodil, Tigerli und Bigboy in der Lokstadt: www.hochparterre.ch, 08.09.2017
	Dominique Boudet (Hg.): Wohngenossenschaften in Zürich, Gartenstädte und neue Nachbarschaften (Wohnüberbauung am Katzenbach III–V, Wohnsiedlungen Brüggliäcker, Schwamendinger-Dreieck und Toblerstrasse), Zürich 2017
	Heinz Wirz und Christoph Wieser (Hg.): Zürcher Wohnungsbau 1995–2015 (Wohnsiedlung Brüggliäcker, Wohnüberbauungen am Katzenbach IV und Guggach), Luzern 2017
2018	Selbstverwaltetes Wohnen (Lokstadt). In: Bau&Architektur 3/2018, S. 13
	Manuel Pestalozzi: Verdichtung am Zürichberg (Wohnsiedlung Toblerstrasse). In: Bau&Architektur 3/2018, S. 4–6
	Parzelle geschickt genutzt (Wohnsiedlung Riedacker). In: Wohnen 9/2018, S. 5
	Andres Herzog: Gemeinsam stark. Von der Arbeitsgemeinschaft bis zur Bürofusion. In: Hochparterre 3/2018, S. 42ff.
	Adam Jasper (Hg.): House Tour. Views of the Unfurnished Interior (Wohnsiedlung Brüggliäcker und Wohnüberbauung am Katzenbach IV), Zürich 2018
	Michael Staub: Weiterbauen am Zürichberg (Wohnsiedlung Toblerstrasse). In: Wohnen 5/2018, S. 27–30
	Heinrich O. Matthias: Wie eine Wohnsiedlung am Zürichberg den anti-urbanen Betonblöcken Paroli bietet (Wohnsiedlung Toblerstrasse): www.nzz.ch, 02.05.2018
2019	Marcel Elsener: Rorschach wird wieder zur Stadt (Feldmühle-Areal Rorschach). In: St. Galler Tagblatt, 05.03.2019, S. 31
	Manuel Pestalozzi: Nutzungswandel in Rorschach (Feldmühle-Areal Rorschach): www.swiss-architects.com, 25.02.2019

TIBOR JOANELLY (TEXTBEITRAG)

1967	geboren in Zürich
1988–1993	Architekturstudium an der ETH Zürich, Diplom bei Prof. Flora Ruchat-Roncati
1993–2000	Reisen in Europa, Arbeit u. a. bei Prof. Miroslav Šik und NOSE Design
1995–1996	Assistent an der Ungarischen Technischen Hochschule Budapest
1997–	Publizistische Tätigkeit
2000–	Selbstständige Tätigkeit als Architekt
2000–2005	Assistent an der ETH Zürich bei Prof. Meinrad Morger, Prof. Andrea Deplazes und Assistenzprof. Christian Kerez
2005–2007	Dozent für Bauentwurfslehre und Architekturtheorie an der Universität Liechtenstein, Vaduz
2007–	Dozent für Architekturtheorie und -kritik, ZHAW Winterthur
2007–2009	Mitarbeit bei atelier ww Zürich
2009–	Redaktor bei werk, bauen + wohnen

CHRISTOPH BAUMBERGER (TEXTBEITRAG)

1971	geboren in Zürich
1987–1991	Ausbildung als Hochbauzeichner
1992–1995	Kantonale Maturitätsschule für Erwachsene
1996–2002	Studium der Philosophie und Germanistik an der Universität Zürich und der Ludwig-Maximilian-Universität München
2001–2009	Assistent am Philosophischen Seminar der Universität Zürich
2003–2005	Dozent an der Hochschule für Gestaltung und Kunst Zürich
2005–2009	Doktorat in Philosophie an der Universität Zürich
2009–	Oberassistent am Institut für Umweltentscheidungen der ETH Zürich
2010–2013	Mitglied des Ethik-Zentrums der Universität Zürich
2018	Habilitation in Philosophie an der Universität Bern
2014–	Dozent im MAS Kulturmanagement der Universität Basel
2016	Gastwissenschaftler an der Free University of Amsterdam
2017	Gastwissenschaftler an der London School of Economics and Political Science
2017–	Dozent im CAS International Policy and Advocacy der Swiss School of Public Governance

2010	"Ersatz einer Siedlung in Zürich Seebach" (Am Katzenbach III housing estate). In: *Neue Zürcher Zeitung*, 23.3.2010
	"Neue Wohnungen am Katzenbach". In: *Tages-Anzeiger*, 15.3.2010, p. 19
2011	Martin Tschanz: "Kultivierte Wohnlichkeit" (Segantini apartment building). In: *werk, bauen + wohnen* 12/2011, p. 58–59
	Ivo Bösch: "Die stillen Gewinner. Ein Architektenteam gewinnt sechs Wohnbauwettbewerbe. In: *Hochparterre* 5/2011, p. 44–45
	Paul Knüsel: "Gartenstadt reloaded" (Am Katzenbach III–V housing estate). In: *faktor* 29/2011, p. 8–10
2012	David Ganzoni: "Wie liest man einen Grundrissplan? Die Gute Wohnung" (Brüggliäcker housing development). In: *Wohnen* 5/2012, p. 26–29
	"Leben mit Ecken und Kanten" (Segantini apartment building). In: *Sonntags Zeitung*, 29.3.2012, p. 63
2013	P. Popp: "Subtile Raumbildung: Schulhaus und Gemeindebibliothek in Dietlikon", at: www.detail.de, 17.12.2013
2014	Richard Liechti: "Mit Bedacht verdichtet" (Brüggliäcker housing estate). In: *Wohnen* 11/2014, S. 22–25
	A. Kohne: "Die Gartenstadt für morgen" (Schwamendinger-Dreieck housing estate). In: *TEC21* 45/2014, p. 8–10
	"Schulhaus Laufen" In: *AS Schweizer Architektur* 195 4/2014, p. 7–10
	"Grundrissfibel Alterszentren 44 Architekturwettbewerbe in der Schweiz 2002–2014". In: *Edition Hochparterre* 2014
	Andres Herzog: "Zickzack unter dem Kostendach" (Laufen school building). In: *Hochparterre* 3/2014, p. 22–26
	Roland Züger: "Vom Dorf ein Bild machen" (Dietlikon school building). In: *werk, bauen + wohnen*, 1/2 2014
2015	Marcel Bächtiger: "Rhetorik und Realität" (competition, Geroldswil centre development), at: www.hochparterre.ch, 19.08.2015
	"Grundrissfibel Schulbauten 30 Wettbewerbe in der Schweiz 2001–2015" (Laufen school building, Blumenfeld school facility). In: *Edition Hochparterre* 2015
2016	Marianne Kürsteiner: "Conserver son caractère à l'image de la ville-jardin" (Brüggliäcker housing estate). In: *idea* 6/2016, p. 46–49
	Christophe Joud: Porte, "Une scénographie des passages" (Brüggliäcker housing estate). In: *cahier de théorie, A l'intérieur*, 13/2016, p. 79–91
	Christian Inderbitzin and Elli Mosayebi: "La porte, une échelle de l'habitat." In: *matières* 13/2016, p. 86–97
	"Schulhausanlage Dietlikon". In: *Lignum Construction bois – Ecoles*, 14/2016, p. 46/47
	Agnès Laube and Michael Widrig: *Archigrafie, Schrift am Bau* (Dietlikon school building), Birkhäuser Verlag 2016
	Emma Letizia Jones and Philip Shelley: "How housing co-operatives built a city" (Brüggliäcker housing estate, competition, Zollstrasse housing and commercial development), at: www.architectural-review.com, 4.10.2016
2017	Werner Huber: "Krokodil, Tigerli und Bigboy in der Lokstadt", at: www.hochparterre.ch, 8.9.2017
	Dominique Boudet (Ed.): *Wohngenossenschaften in Zürich, Gartenstädte und neue Nachbarschaften* (Am Katzenbach III–V housing developments, Brüggliäcker housing estate, Schwamendinger-Dreieck housing estate and Toblerstrasse housing estate], Park Books 2017
	Heinz Wirz and Christoph Wieser (Eds.): *Zürcher Wohnungsbau* 1995–2015 (Brüggliäcker housing estate, Am Katzenbach IV housing development and Guggach housing development), Quart Verlag 2017
2018	"Selbstverwaltetes Wohnen" (Lokstadt). In: *Bau&Architektur* 3/2018, p. 13
	Manuel Pestalozzi: "Verdichtung am Zürichberg" (Toblerstr. housing estate). In: *Bau&Architektur* 3/2018, p. 4–6
	"Parzelle geschickt genutzt" (Riedacker housing estate). In: *Wohnen* 9/2018, p. 5
	Andres Herzog: "Gemeinsam stark. Von der Arbeitsgemeinschaft bis zur Bürofusion." In: *Hochparterre* 3/2018, p. 42ff
	Adam Jasper (Ed.): *House Tour: Views of the Unfurnished Interior* (Brüggliäcker housing estate and Am Katzenbach IV housing development), Park Books 2018
	Michael Staub: "Weiterbauen am Zürichberg" (Toblerstrasse housing estate). In: *Wohnen* 5/2018, p. 27–30
	Heinrich O. Matthias: "Wie eine Wohnsiedlung am Zürichberg den anti-urbanen Betonblöcken Paroli bietet" (Toblerstrasse housing estate), at: www.nzz.ch, 2.5.2018
2019	Marcel Elsener: "Rorschach wird wieder zur Stadt" (Feldmühle-Areal Rorschach). In: *St. Galler Tagblatt*, 5.3.2019, p. 31
	Manuel Pestalozzi: "Nutzungswandel in Rorschach" (Feldmühle-Areal Rorschach), at: www.swiss-architects.com, 25.2.2019

TIBOR JOANELLY (ARTICLE)

1967	Born in Zurich
1988–1993	Studied Architecture at the ETH Zurich, graduating under Prof. Flora Ruchat-Roncati
1993–2000	Travels, employers including Miroslav Šik and NOSE Design
1995–1996	Assistant at the Technical University of Budapest, Hungary
1997–	Publisher
2000–	Freelance work
2000–2005	Assistant at the ETH Zurich under Meinrad Morger, Andrea Deplazes and Christian Kerez
2005–2007	Lecturer in Building Design and Architectural Theory, University of Liechtenstein
2007–	Lecturer in Architectural Theory and Critique, ZHAW Winterthur
2007–2009	Employed at atelier ww, Zurich
2009–	Editor at *werk, bauen + wohnen*

CHRISTOPH BAUMBERGER (ARTICLE)

1971	Born in Zurich
1987–1991	Apprenticeship as a draughtsman
1992–1995	Kantonale Maturitätsschule für Erwachsene
1996–2002	Studied Philosophy and German, University of Zurich and Ludwig-Maximilian-Universität München
2001–2009	Assistant at the Philosophy Seminar, University of Zurich
2003–2005	Lecturer at the Zurich University of the Arts
2005–2009	Doctorate in Philosophy at the University of Zurich
2009–	Senior Assistant, Institute of Environmental Decisions, ETH Zurich
2010–2013	Member of the Ethics Centre, University of Zurich
2018	Habilitation in Philosophy, University of Bern
2014–	Lecturer, MAS Cultural Management, University of Basel
2016	Guest Researcher, Free University of Amsterdam
2017	Guest Researcher, London School of Economics and Political Science
2017–	Lecturer, CAS International Policy and Advocacy at the Swiss School of Public Governance

FINANZIELLE UND IDEELLE UNTERSTÜTZUNG

FINANCIAL AND CONCEPTUAL SUPPORT

Ein besonderer Dank gilt den Institutionen und Sponsorfirmen, deren finanzielle Unterstützungen wesentlich zum Entstehen dieser Buchreihe beitragen. Ihr kulturelles Engagement ermöglicht ein fruchtbares und freundschaftliches Zusammenwirken von Baukultur und Bauwirtschaft.

Special thanks to our sponsors and institutions whose financial support has helped us so much with the production of this series of books. Their cultural commitment is a valuable contribution to fruitful and cordial collaboration between the culture and economics of architecture.

pro helvetia

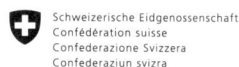
Schweizerische Eidgenossenschaft
Confédération suisse
Confederazione Svizzera
Confederaziun svizra

Eidgenössisches Departement des Innern EDI
Bundesamt für Kultur BAK

Böni Gebäudetechnik AG, Oberentfelden

Buchmann Partner AG, Uster

Clienia AG Privatklinikgruppe, Winterthur

EBP Schweiz AG, Zürich

ewp Gruppe, Effretikon

Hinderer Liegenschaften AG, Oetwil am See

Implenia Schweiz AG, Dietlikon

Steiner AG, Zürich

Versicherungsberatung für KMU GmbH, Dübendorf

Wichser Akustik & Bauphysik AG, Zürich

wlw Bauingenieure AG, Zürich/Mels/Fläsch

Anliker AG Bauunternehmung, Thalwil
Fenster Nauer AG, Samstagern
Genossenschaft für Wohnkultur, Muri AG
Planpartner AG, Zürich
Stiftung PWG, Zürich

Baumberger & Stegmeier
83. Band der Reihe De aedibus
Herausgeber: Heinz Wirz, Luzern
Konzept: Heinz Wirz; Baumberger & Stegmeier, Zürich
Projektleitung: Quart Verlag, Antonia Chavez-Wirz
Textbeiträge: Tibor Joanelly, Christoph Baumberger
Objekttexte: Baumberger & Stegmeier
Lektorat (dt.): Kirsten Rachowiak, München
Übersetzung Deutsch–Englisch: Benjamin Liebelt, Berlin
Fotos: Baumberger & Stegmeier, Zürich S. 6–11, 27, 32 M., 48 u., 62, 64 u.; David K. Ross, Montreal S. 12; Stiftung Preußische Schlösser und Gärten Berlin-Brandenburg, Potsdam S. 14 o.; Roland Bernath, Zürich S. 14 u., 15–17, 19, 21, 23–26, 29–31, 33–35, 37, 39, 41, 42 u., 43, 45, 46 M. & u., 47, 49, 51–53; Chen Kuen Lee, Stuttgart S. 18 o.; Akademie der Künste Berlin, Sammlung Baukunst, Berlin S. 18 u.; strüwing reklamefoto, Kopenhagen S. 22 l.; Museum Laufental, Sammlung Schaltenbrand, Laufen S. 22 M. u.; fahrländer scherrer, Zürich S. 28 o.; Baugeschichtliches Archiv, Zürich S. 32 l. o., 54 o.; Freilichtmuseum Ballenberg, Hofstetten bei Brienz S. 32 l. u.; Walter Binder, Zürich S. 36; P. Ayrault, Inventaire général, ADAGP, Paris S. 42 o.; Reto Führer, Felsberg S. 46 o.; Luis García S. 48 o.; Jürg Zimmermann, Zürich S. 55, 57; Archiv FHNW, Windisch S. 56; Christoph Baumberger, Zollikon S. 66–73
Visualisierungen und Pläne: Baumberger & Stegmeier
Redesign: BKVK, Basel – Beat Keusch, Angelina Köpplin-Stützle
Grafische Umsetzung: Quart Verlag Luzern
Lithos: Printeria, Luzern
Druck: DZA Druckerei zu Altenburg GmbH, Altenburg

© Copyright 2020
Quart Verlag Luzern, Heinz Wirz
Alle Rechte vorbehalten
ISBN 978-3-03761-097-8

Baumberger & Stegmeier
Volume 83 of the series De aedibus
Edited by: Heinz Wirz, Lucerne
Concept: Heinz Wirz; Baumberger & Stegmeier, Zurich
Project management: Quart Verlag, Antonia Chavez-Wirz
Articles by: Christoph Baumberger, Tibor Joanelly
Project descriptions: Baumberger & Stegmeier
German text editing: Kirsten Rachowiak, Munich
German–English translation: Benjamin Liebelt, Berlin
Photos: Baumberger & Stegmeier, Zurich p. 6–11, 27, 32 m., 48 b., 62, 64 b.; David K. Ross, Montreal p. 12; Stiftung Preußische Schlösser und Gärten Berlin-Brandenburg, Potsdam p. 14 t.; Roland Bernath, Zurich p. 14 b., 15–17, 19, 21, 23–26, 29–31, 33–35, 37, 39, 41, 42 b., 43, 45, 46 m. & b., 47, 49, 51–53; Chen Kuen Lee, Stuttgart p. 18 t.; Akademie der Künste Berlin, Sammlung Baukunst, Berlin p. 18 b.; strüwing reklamefoto, Copenhagen p. 22 l.; Museum Laufental, Sammlung Schaltenbrand, Laufen p. 22 m. b.; fahrländer scherrer, Zurich p. 28 t.; Baugeschichtliches Archiv, Zurich p. 32 l. t., 54 t.; Freilichtmuseum Ballenberg, Hofstetten bei Brienz p. 32 l. b.; Walter Binder, Zurich p. 36; P. Ayrault, Inventaire général, ADAGP, Paris p. 42 t.; Reto Führer, Felsberg p. 46 t.; Luis García p. 48 t.; Jürg Zimmermann, Zurich p. 55, 57; Archiv FHNW, Windisch p. 56; Christoph Baumberger, Zollikon p. 66–73
Graphics and plans: Baumberger & Stegmeier
Redesign: BKVK, Basel – Beat Keusch, Angelina Köpplin-Stützle
Graphic design: Quart Verlag Lucerne
Lithos: Printeria, Lucerne
Printing: DZA Druckerei zu Altenburg GmbH, Altenburg

© Copyright 2020
Quart Verlag Luzern, Heinz Wirz
All rights reserved
ISBN 978-3-03761-097-8

De aedibus
Zeitgenössische Architekten und ihre Bauten

De aedibus
Contemporary architects and their buildings

83	Baumberger & Stegmeier (de/en)	42	Durisch + Nolli (de/en)
82	L-architectes (de/en, de/fr)	41	sabarchitekten (de/en)
81	Frei Rezakhanlou (de/en)	40	Beat Rothen (de/en)
80	weberbrunner (de/en)	39	Atelier Bonnet (de/en)
79	Meyer Piattini (de/en)	38	Novaron (de/en)
78	meier + associés architectes (de/en, de/fr)	37	Althammer Hochuli (de/en)
77	Lin Robbe Seiler (de/en, de/fr)	36	Schneider & Schneider (de/en)
76	Meier Leder (de/en)	35	Frei & Ehrensperger (de und en)
75	Butikofer de Oliveira Vernay (de/en)	34	Liechti Graf Zumsteg (de/en)
74	Elisabeth & Martin Boesch (de/en)	33	Adrian Streich (de/en)
73	spaceshop Architekten (de/en)	32	Daniele Marques (de/en)
72	Kast Kaeppeli (de/en)	31	Neff Neumann (de/en)
71	Philippe Meyer (de/en, fr)	30	Giraudi Wettstein (de/en)
70	bartbuchhofer (de/en)	29	Steinmann & Schmid (de/en)
69	Hauenstein La Roche Schedler (de/en)	28	Matthias Ackermann (de/en)
68	Graeme Mann & Patricia Capua Mann (de/en)	27	Aeby & Perneger (de/en)
67	Esposito Javet (de/en und de/fr)	26	Bakker & Blanc (de/en)
66	Galletti Matter (de/en und de/fr)	25	Markus Wespi Jérôme de Meuron (de/en)
65	Fruehauf, Henry & Viladoms (de/en)	24	Bauart (de/en und de/fr)
64	Jakob Steib (de/en)	23	Knapkiewicz & Fickert (de/en)
63	bunq (de/en)	22	Marcel Ferrier (de/en)
62	Jean-Paul Jaccaud (de/en und de/fr)	21	Wild Bär Architekten (de/en)
61	huggenbergerfries (de/en)	20	Enzmann + Fischer (de/en)
60	Berrel Berrel Kräutler (de/en)	19	Mierta und Kurt Lazzarini (de/en)
59	Pierre-Alain Dupraz (de/en und de/fr)	18	Rolf Mühlethaler (de/en)
58	Cometti Truffer (de/en)	17	Pablo Horváth (de/en)
57	Joos & Mathys (de/en)	16	Brauen + Wälchli (de/en)
56	Lacroix Chessex (de/en)	15	E2A Eckert Eckert Architekten (de/en)
55	Savioz Fabrizzi (de/en und de/fr)	14	Lussi + Halter (de/en)
54	Boegli Kramp (de/en)	13	Philipp Brühwiler (de/en)
53	Zita Cotti (de/en)	12	Scheitlin – Syfrig + Partner (de/en)
52	Oestreich + Schmid (de/en)	11	Vittorio Magnago Lampugnani (de/en)
51	Stump & Schibli Architekten (de/en)	10	Bonnard Woeffray (de/en und de/fr)
50	Luca Gazzaniga (de/en)	9	Graber Pulver (de/en)
49	Guignard & Saner (de/en)	8	Burkhalter Sumi / Makiol Wiederkehr (de/en)
48	Morger + Dettli (de/en)	7	Gigon/Guyer (de und en)
47	Charles Pictet (de/en)	6	Andrea Bassi (de, fr und en)
46	Armando Ruinelli + Partner (de/en/it)	5	Dieter Jüngling und Andreas Hagmann (de und en)
45	Luca Selva Architekten (de/en)	4	Beat Consoni (de und en)
44	Luca Deon (de/en)	3	Max Bosshard & Christoph Luchsinger (de)
43	2b (de/en)	2	Miroslav Šik (de, en und it)
		1	Valentin Bearth & Andrea Deplazes (de, en und it)

books@quart.ch, www.quart.ch